W9-AFS-358

To the *Purchaser*

of this Book, from its Publisher:—

ALL PAPER, *including the paper on which books are printed, as well as the materials which go into the manufacture of paper are absolutely essential to the prosecution of the war.*

§§ Because of this, book publishers are now seriously restricted in the amount of paper which is available for books. For 1944 my firm is allowed but three-quarters as many pounds of paper as we used in the calendar year of 1942.

§§ This means that unless we economize in the use of paper in every way possible, we shall not be able to print anything like all of the books readers will demand of us. This is particularly important because our list abounds in good books published as long as twenty years ago (the Borzoi was founded in 1915) for which there is still steady demand and which we do not wish to let go out of print.

§§ We are therefore reducing the size of our books and also their thickness, and have made an effort, without sacrificing readability, to reduce the number of pages by getting more printed matter on each page. For this we must beg your indulgence, though I think that in many ways the smaller and thinner books are more attractive to handle and to read than their larger and fatter fellows. On the other hand, despite the shortage of all materials that go into the making of books and the critical manpower shortage among all printers and binders, we intend in every way possible to preserve those physical qualities which have long made Borzoi Books outstanding. We will use cloths of as good quality as we can procure and will maintain the same high standards of typographical and binding design.

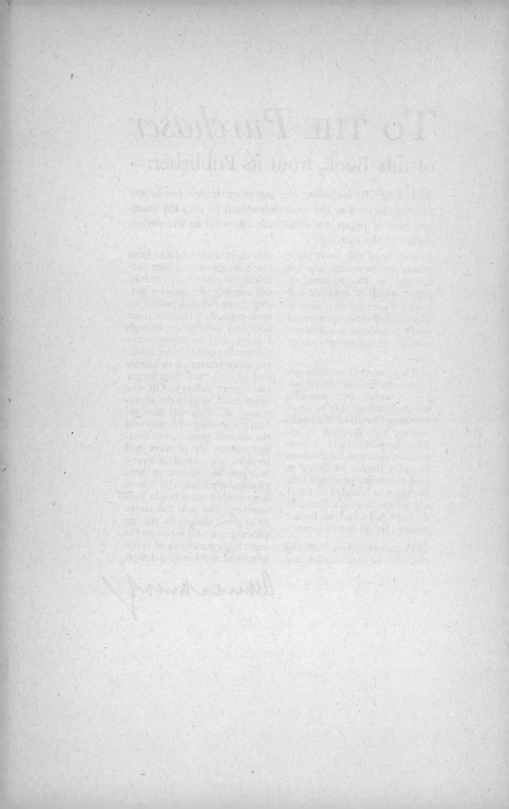

Music and *Musicians*

MASTERS OF RUSSIAN MUSIC
by *M. D. Calvocoressi and Gerald Abraham*

CHARLES T. GRIFFES by *Edward M. Maisel*

BRAHMS by *Walter Niemann*

THE LIFE OF RICHARD WAGNER by *Ernest Newman*

MOUSSORGSKY by *Otto von Riesemann*

MY MUSICAL LIFE by *Nikolay Andreyevich Rimsky-Korsakov*

DMITRI SHOSTAKOVICH The Life and Background of a Soviet
Composer by *Victor Ilyich Seroff*

BEETHOVEN: HIS SPIRITUAL DEVELOPMENT
by *J. W. N. Sullivan*

MANUEL DE FALLA AND SPANISH MUSIC
by *J. B. Trend*

MOZART by *W. J. Turner*

TCHAIKOVSKY by *Herbert Weinstock*

THE BOOK OF MODERN COMPOSERS
edited by *David Ewen*

These are BORZOI BOOKS, *published by* Alfred A. Knopf

Bohuslav Martinů

BOHUSLAV MARTINŮ

THE MAN
AND HIS MUSIC

BY

MILOŠ ŠAFRÁNEK

ALFRED A. KNOPF : NEW YORK

1944

Published simultaneously in Canada by The Ryerson Press

Manufactured in the United States of America

FIRST EDITION

TO THE MEMORY
OF MY MOTHER

Table of Contents

TABLE OF CONTENTS

List of Illustrations

Acknowledgments

SOME of the material in this book has already been published in my article on Bohuslav Martinů in the *Musical Quarterly*, Vol. XXIX, No. 3, July 1943, to which I wish to express my appreciation for permission to reprint.

I also wish to acknowledge the invaluable help of Rebecca Clarke in her revision of the English text. And my warm thanks are due to Mrs. Božena Linhartová, who most kindly translated the Czech text into English.

Mrs. Martinů was also very helpful to me in checking the dates of her husband's compositions.

M. Š.

Introduction

IT is a real adventure, discouraging and at the same time hopeful, to be placed by the circumstances of one's life and work in the midst of an epoch that is at once so chaotic and so full of promise as the first half of the present century.

That the modern world is sick, that everything is in a condition of disintegration, and that the present moral crisis threatens to bury all human values has been said so often that it is a platitude. The thirty-year war which started in 1914 has brought the entire world into turmoil and changed all material and spiritual values. It is as though mankind were waiting for leaders to convert this chaos into order and unity. Perhaps the most characteristic sign of the upheaval is that it has deeply affected the arts, which in many ways have felt its influence sooner than political, social and economic institutions. This is due to the fact that culture, by its very nature, reacts spontaneously and sensitively to all changes in the human sphere. In music such a crisis was felt in the days of exaggerated romanticism, in which there was, to quote Brahms's words about Bruckner, "not a shimmer of musical logic, no idea of orderly musical construction," and everything was "affected, nothing natural." The reaction to these extremes — which had brought music to a virtual dead end — began, in France, with Debussy, and reached its height in the 1920's. Since that time all music has been a protest against the excessive individualism that is, as John Dewey puts it, "the monopolization of spiritual capital." Composers have felt very strongly that in an era in which music was becoming the most social of arts, heard by millions of people through the medium of concerts and radio, they must not again isolate themselves from the rest of the world. For isolationism, which in the political and economic spheres has resulted in the misery of two world wars, might easily cause the overthrow of all music and art. Furthermore, great discoveries in the sciences such as physics, biology, and anthropology have brought so much exhilarating inspiration to artists and philosophers that the composer now has greater freedom than ever to become an integral part of the world as a whole.

Martinů's life has been a continual struggle for the creation of an art in line with the problems of today. Ever since his maturity, during his seventeen years' sojourn in Paris as well as since the time of his arrival in the United States in 1941, he has continued patiently and with iron determination to adapt his music to a human language. From early youth he has been repelled by all excessive individualism. True, he was born in a tower, completely isolated from the outside world. But instead of shutting himself away in an ivory tower he has learned to look upon human weaknesses with the indulgence of a bird's-eye point of view, and to differentiate between them and the more permanent qualities of man. His inborn dislike of sentimentality has been confirmed by studies and observations. While still in his formative years, when he was a violinist in the Czech Philharmonic Orchestra in Prague, Martinů found himself in complete disagreement with the one-sided æsthetics of the time, emphasizing as they did the literary and philosophical aspect of music rather than its form. Debussy with his new harmonic sense was a great revelation to him at that period. Martinů's special love for the music of the sixteenth, seventeenth, and eighteenth centuries — Orlando di Lasso, Palestrina, Bach, Mozart — is due not only to an appreciation of its timeless perfection but also to the fact that he finds it to have a practical human purpose. With Nietzsche he despises all hostility to life as a sign of effeminacy, decadence, and histrionism; and he longs to feel himself at one with the world. He has never been afflicted by *"la terreur du lieu commun"* — that fear of the commonplace which, as the

French writer Jean Schlumberger says, must inevitably leave a vacuum in art in the very place where it should be common to all mankind. Martinů himself has said, in the program notes for his First Symphony: "What I maintain as my deepest conviction is the essential nobility of thoughts and things which are quite simple. . . ."

The exaggerated artistic manifestations of the chaotic period between the two world wars — the early 1920's in particular — inspired Martinů with skepticism and distrust; he well knew that they would have but a short life. And he heartily disliked the prevalent obsession with novelty at any price. In spite of this his work contains many new elements, often anticipating by some years the trend of modern music. On the other hand, his high respect for all that has been great in music through the centuries failed to make a neo-classicist of him, although this was the prevailing fashion of the 1920's. His compositions are in a manner of his own, having no relation to current fashions. In this connection it is interesting to note that he is to a large extent self-taught, never having found a school or movement which satisfied him. His strongest interest has always been in Czech folklore. What he was continually seeking was the golden mean that should make music comprehensible to all. And in the whole of his mature work — his operas, his orchestral compositions, and his chamber music — he comes as close as anyone else to expressing the feelings of his fellow man. His music, though at first glance complicated, is in reality natural and spontaneous. He has simply — to quote Goethe's famous sentence about Raphael — "done what the rest of the world would have liked to do."

There is a certain similarity between Raphael's time and today. Raphael immortalized two traditions: the beauty of the antique world, and the Christian humanism of his time. He lived in the days of the great popes, who were also great humanists; the realization of the essential oneness of classical culture and Christian tradition was but a step away. But it was Raphael alone who attained this synthesis in his work. Temperate in expression, he was much less brilliant and sensational than the famous quatrocentists. His work is almost all that remains to us of this unique synthesis in history; for the dawning reconciliation between Platonic and Christian ethics was destroyed by the Nordic barbarism of the French invasion of Italy. This was followed by the period of Spanish pilfering and fanaticism which culminated in the Inquisition, still further frustrating the possibility of any harmony of thought.

Is not the artist of today witnessing similar events? Nordic barbarism, oppression, and the outcries of false prophets are attempting to demolish civilization, which nevertheless resolutely continues to follow the pattern of a new humanism. Will this period — with its new relational conceptions of the world which have been presented by the scientific humanists — find the artist ready for worthy accomplishment? This is the problem which faces the composer of the present time. And Bohuslav Martinů — as I shall try to show in this book — is creating for this new world with perseverance and also with success. He would be the last, however, to claim for himself any exalted position; he does not aspire to be more than a modest workman in the cause of contemporary art. As he himself says: "I do not perform any miracles. I am merely exact."

In regard to the literary method of this book I feel, because of my love for the subject, that it belongs to some extent in the province of Boswelliana. I mention the name of Boswell with great reserve, however, for in spite of my long friendship with Martinů I have never taken down any of our conversations. It was my unexpected reunion with Martinů in America that supplied the final impulse to the materialization of our many discussions. During the writing of an article on Martinů and the planning of this book a friendly check-up between the two of us began. There were many free cross-examinations, of which the most intimate took place during the summer of 1943 in Martinů's cottage on Good-Wives River Road in Darien, as well as on the Compo Cove Beach in Westport. For all æsthetic conclusions — the description of the composer's creative process in particular — personal notes, which Martinů jotted down in a little notebook, were relied on. These jotting would be a puzzle to any inquisitive reader; they are very laconic and have no orderly sequence. I merely used them as signposts in the broad context of my experience of the composer, whose career I have followed step by step — in sketches, in scores, in performances, and in almost daily talks — since 1927. Light has also been thrown on Martinů's mental processes by the remarks written on the margins of books that he has read. For instance, certain passages are marked with a treble clef, indicating that the composer found in what he was reading an analogy with the field of music or art in general.

If it were not for our long friendship this book could hardly have been attempted. Martinů is no conversationalist. He is immoderately shy and modest, and it is very difficult to get him to talk about himself, still more so about his music. Curiously enough, there is practically no literature about him in existence,[1] apart, of course, from an enormous mass of newspaper criticism of his work. Even such a valuable book as Aaron Copland's *Our New Music*, published in 1941, does not mention his name, though the omission was naturally not deliberate. Musical dictionaries and encyclopedias give incomplete and often inaccurate information on the subject of his

---

[1] To be exact, the following articles on Martinů should be mentioned: Pierre-Octave Ferroud's "A Great Musician of Today: B. Martinů" in the *Chesterian*, Vol. XVII, No. 122, March–April 1937; two articles by me: "Summing Up Martinů's Output," in the *New York Times*, June 18, 1939; and "Bohuslav Martinů," in the *Musical Quarterly*, Vol. XXIX, No. 3, July 1943; and an essay by Paul Nettl in *The Book of Modern Composers*, edited by David Ewen (New York: Alfred A. Knopf; 1942).

career. It is not even possible to study his compositions by means of phonograph records, as, strangely enough, out of over a hundred works recordings have been made of only two. But, when all is said and done, Martinů has never allowed his fame to make him into an official personality; he has been too busy with the work that inspired him.

This book, then, is the fruit of a long, close friendship, which has included many difficult times as well as many happy ones; of pleasant idle strolls along the quais of the Seine, and of meetings and talks in America. As in every real friendship, there has never been any desire on either side to take advantage of the abilities of the other. No literary purpose — such as that of Ackermann and Goethe — has for a moment thrown its shadow on our relations. Our friendship has been strengthened by common ideals and hopes, and grows firmer in the approaching light of a happier future. It may be that the very diversity of our professions has contributed to it. What is essential, however, is our parallel struggle towards a new and better world.

M. Š.

COMPO COVE, WESTPORT, CONNECTICUT
October 1943

Bohuslav Martinů

Part I
Childhood and Preparation

1 : In the Tower

ONE of the keys to the singularly detached quality of Bohuslav Martinů's work and personality is the curious circumstance that he was born and brought up in the tower of a country church. There, a hundred feet above the rest of the world, he lived with his family in almost complete isolation for the first thirteen years of his life. Two hundred steps of a dark winding staircase were his only means of descending to the town, to people, to reality. And he used these but seldom.

Ever since the day when Sainte-Beuve gave a metaphorical interpretation to Alfred de Vigny's poem *La Tour d'ivoire* poets and romantics of all kinds have taken refuge in towers — metaphorical ivory towers — in order to escape the trivialities of real life and give themselves up to their dreams. Martinů, however, arrived in his tower under quite simple and unromantic conditions. His parents had been living there for years; his father, Ferdinand Martinů, in addition to practicing the honest trade of a shoemaker, was employed as keeper of the tower in the Church of St. Jacob on the Little Square in Polička, a small town in eastern Bohemia, where his duties included taking care of the bells and watching for fires in the

MARTINŮ'S BIRTHPLACE IN POLIČKA

countryside. And there, on December 8, 1890, Bohuslav Martinů was born.

To the child the tower was thus a natural and familiar home, which he shared with his brother and sister František and Marie. The oldest son, Karel, had already left Polička to take up employment in Prague. The children were strictly brought up. Their parents were already past middle age at the time of Bohuslav's birth, and the mother, an energetic housekeeper, was a stern and domineering woman who often treated him very severely. But the child's normal need for affection was satisfied by his father, a gentle, kindly man with a great love of nature, which expressed itself in the quantities of bright-colored flowers that he carefully grew and tended on top of his church tower.

From the stone parapet which encircled the tower just under their windows the Martinů family looked out, from one year's end to another, upon a considerable expanse of the surrounding countryside. There were blue woods on the horizon — peaceful woods, friendly rather than romantic; and the pure white vista of winter, when for four long months the ground was covered with snow; and a kaleidoscope of tiny fields, cultivated with neatness and love by the small Czech farmers. From his earliest age little Bohuslav never tired of peering through the star-shaped apertures with which the parapet was decorated and of running from one to another to discover new views of the world below, all framed by these openings. The vast Czech countryside, beautiful in its clarity and simplicity, has in itself something at once modest, shy, and deeply inspiring, bearing spiritual traces of its historic past. To Bohuslav it often seemed as though the change of the seasons — the arrival of spring, the summer storms, with their lightning and thunder, the autumn winds, and the winter snows — reached him at first hand, direct from heaven, before the little antlike people on the earth below received them. But even these elements were always clearly etched, entirely without any veil of romantic mist, because in the dry climate of this country fogs are almost unknown.

To the boy in the tower the details of life in the town below were naturally not visible. For him humanity could attain significance only when it involved large groups of people, such as funeral processions winding slowly from the church to the cemetery outside the town; or weddings and other peasant festivities; or the occasional military maneuvers, which to him appeared like a game of animated toy soldiers, with little cannon, horses, and wagons. But on Sundays and holidays and nearly every week-day morning the sound of conventional organ music and the singing of churchgoers were wafted up to him. And the rhythmical passing of time, its every second, was ceaselessly marked by the ticking of the large tower clock.

It was not until Martinů was six years old that he started regularly to go down to the town to attend school. His first daily contact with other children and with ordinary life in Polička had now begun.[1] At this time, too, he made his first practical acquaintance with music, for he started to take violin

---

[1] The town of Polička — which in Martinů's youth had about 5,000 inhabitants, mainly small farmers, shoemakers, and weavers — is situated on the Bohemian-Moravian mountain range in eastern Bohemia, near Moravia, to which it really belongs. This is why Martinů so often stresses the fact that he comes from Moravia rather than Bohemia, thus claiming a closer affinity with the folklore of the Moravian peasants. As can be seen by the ruins of the fort — founded in 1265 by the Czech King Přemysl Otakar II as a business and trade center — it is a historical place. Soon after its establishment it became a King's Dowager town. The inhabitants of these towns were generally free, being subject only to the King, who saw to it through his officials that the income of the town flowed directly into the State Treasury. There were, however, many occasions for the citizens to participate in the Citizens Council and Judiciary. These King's Dowager towns were strongly affected by the Hussite movement, and there are still in the vicinity of Polička secret paths used by the outlawed brethren, as well as other remains of this famous period in the history of Bohemia. Polička soon extricated itself from the rule of the King's officers; but after the Battle of the White Mountain, in 1620, it was deprived of all privileges and estates, which were later returned only to citizens of the Roman Catholic faith. This was the reason why so many of its citizens moved to foreign countries, and the town was slowly dwindling. Polička also had two disastrous fires, one in 1613, the other in 1845. To this day the town inside the fortifications is a special community, owning property for which special taxes are paid,

4

lessons from the local tailor, Mr. Černovský. There was nothing unusual in this, though it proved to be such an important step in Martinů's life. He simply, like most children of his age, began to take music lessons, and twice a week, together with four or five other youngsters, was taught the violin by Mr. Černovský. And as his home did not furnish him with many diversions, he practiced very diligently just for his own amusement.

At school he did not get on very well, being particularly weak in drawing and mathematics. It was not easy for him to make friends with the other children. He was a very shy little boy, silent and completely engrossed in his own thoughts; and only gradually was he able to adapt himself to the society of his fellow beings. Daily attendance at morning Mass with all the other school children, however, slowly helped to overcome the effects of his former isolation — at least outwardly. He was now able to watch at close range the folk customs, many of them dating back hundreds of years, which were peculiar to the children of that district; but he was too bashful to take any active part in them. These ceremonies mostly took place in the winter around Christmas-time; and the sight of the shepherds of Bethlehem making the rounds of the town together with an angel and a devil, the Three Kings at Epiphany, and other customs of typical Czech charm became to him deeply rooted memories to which he returned much later in life.

The boy's progress on the violin was exceptionally rapid. At the age of eight he performed compositions by de Bériot and Wieniawski at local concerts. It was just at this time that the Czech violin virtuoso Jan Kubelík was making his first sensational success, and the citizens of Polička longed to be able

---

while those who are not citizens inside the fort have only to pay the town taxes. Martinů's grandfather on his mother's side, who owned a cabinet-maker's shop, was a citizen. At the time of Bohuslav Martinů's childhood there were in Polička about a dozen families bearing that name, none of them related to the composer's family.

to produce a Kubelík of their own. But Bohuslav did not nurse any such ambitions. Even at that time he was more interested in composing than in playing the violin — though, strangely enough, he did not write anything for himself to play. His first composition, for string quartet, was written when he was ten years old; and in this he betrayed his inexperience by writing the viola part in the treble clef. But the work was set down swiftly and without any preliminary sketches. Music paper was expensive, and as his strict mother looked upon it as a needless waste of money, he was obliged to rule his own. Nevertheless, from that time on he never stopped composing.

In addition to his favorite occupation of writing music he was also a great reader. This passion for books has always remained with Martinů. Before the age of sixteen, when he left Polička to go to the Prague Conservatory of Music, he had already read the complete literature of the Czech novel as far as it was accessible to him in the local public library. He was especially fond of the patriotic stories of such popular writers as V. B. Třebizský and Alois Jirásek, in which famous incidents of Czech history are described. František Rubeš, an excellent Czech humorist, was also one of his favorites, and still remains so. Even today Martinů cherishes the idea of composing a work for the theater to one of Rubeš's texts.

The influence of the theater came into his life while he was still very young. His father was the prompter of a local amateur theatrical society which gave several performances every year, and sometimes he would take Bohuslav along with him to rehearsal. There was at that time a beautiful old theater in Polička, now housing the Polička museum. Here the national plays of J. K. Tyl, Klicpera, and Šubrt (pronounced Schubert) were performed; and the season was usually brought to a climax with the drama *Anežka* (*Agnes*), written on a local historical theme by František Zakrejs. At the rehearsals young

MARTINŮ'S BOYHOOD HOME

MARTINŮ'S MOTHER AND FATHER

Bohuslav would sit hour after hour in the cold, dark theater, huddling in his overcoat, completely overcome by all his new impressions. In this way he became familiar in early childhood with the theater "in the making," so to speak; and to his two great interests — musical composition and books — a third was now added. To these he has remained faithful to this day.

2 : Studies in Prague, 1906–13

SEVERAL years before Bohuslav Martinů had reached the age of sixteen, which was required for entrance into the Conservatory of Music in Prague, some well-to-do citizens of Polička had decided to send him there to study the violin and had influenced his father and mother to give their consent for the boy to attend this famous musical institution, then nearly a hundred years old. The parents had in the meanwhile moved down to the square opposite the picturesque rampart gate, and into the house of the Polička Savings Bank; and for two years Bohuslav lived with them there, devoting most of his time to reading and the violin. As soon as he was old enough he took the entrance examination for the Prague Conservatory, passing with high marks, and was assigned to the class of an excellent teacher, Professor Suchý. So the tall, thin, and still shy sixteen-year-old lad left his home and set out for the capital, taking with him a black wooden trunk, such as was used by students at that time, and a bundle containing his feather bed. In Prague he lived the life of a poor student on the seven gulden (about $2.50 in American money, in the value of that time) which he received every month from his parents.

Only slowly and with great difficulty was he able to adapt

7

himself to his new environment. Basically his life did not change very much. But he was now able gradually to widen the scope of his three main interests — composition, books, and the theater. Before long, however, he grew tired of working at the Conservatory, in spite of the fact that he was making good progress with his violin studies as well as in harmony and counterpoint. The strict discipline of the Austrian educational system was contrary to his youthful ideas of independence and personal liberty. But as far as books were concerned, Prague opened a new world for Martinů. At last he was able to get all he wanted. Six times he read through the complete works of Dostoyevsky; also Turgenev, who appealed to him less; and Tolstoy and Goncharov, who appealed to him not at all. About Gogol he was enthusiastic. And, in common with the youth of his time, he discovered the so-called decadent literature, including Strindberg among the Scandinavians and Stanislaw Przybyszewski among the Polish writers. All of these he greatly admired.

During this period his attempts at composition were all closely linked to literature, but none of them were really successful. For instance, after reading Victor Hugo's *Les Travailleurs de la mer*, he made sketches for an ambitious work scored for large orchestra. The novel itself did not particularly appeal to him, but nevertheless it aroused a very strong musical response, the results of which he wrote down on the spur of the moment. This three-page sketch (which in 1938 Martinů discovered hidden away in the attic of his parents' house in Polička) shows that though he already had at that time a genuine feeling for orchestration, his technique was still inadequate; and the work was never finished. Later on he planned to write an opera based on Przybyszewski's *De Profundis*.

Kasimierz Tetmajer's two-part novel *Angel of Death* was another literary work which inspired him to compose a symphonic poem. And he wrote still another composition for orchestra on *La Mort de Tintagiles*, one of three plays for marionettes by Maurice Maeterlinck. This last was seriously considered for performance by Dr. Vilém Zemánek, at that time conductor of the Czech Philharmonic Orchestra. Martinů's first two ballets of this period drew their inspiration from the French poet Albert Samain, some of whose poems he also made use of several years later as the basis for a symphonic triptych. The first ballet lasted sixty minutes and was full of nymphs and fauns. The second ballet, a shorter work, is based on a typical Martinů theme — dual personality, with reflections in a mirror portrayed on the stage by two dancers. The reason he chose ballet for his first scenic works is obvious: he had not at that time mastered the technique of writing for the voice. This remained a problem to him for some years. Nevertheless he was constantly writing during his studies at the Conservatory, and produced a great number of works. Unfortunately most of these have been lost, and Martinů himself remembers hardly any of them. All that he can recall, for instance, of a string quintet which he composed while studying in Prague is the unison opening; and this chiefly because he was taken to task on its account by a certain worthy professor. In fact, the only one of his works of that time which remains in his memory is *Niponari*, a cycle of songs with instrumental accompaniment that he composed on Oriental texts about 1908.

From this period onwards Martinů spent a great deal of time in the theater. If he liked a particular play or opera he would go to see it again and again. In fact it often happened that on a Sunday he would go to three separate performances. Because of his extreme poverty he could afford only the cheapest seats, up in the top gallery. But from there, as from his tower at home, he often gained a better general view by being able to look down upon the entire panorama of the theater beneath him.

9

The Prague theater had a very high standard at that time. Connoisseurs came from all over Europe to attend the performances of Shakespeare given at the National Theater, with Edvard Vojan in the principal parts. The operatic productions, under Karel Kovařovič, were also held in high esteem. The Czech public is devoted to the theater, which plays a large part in the national life. The most enthusiastic patrons of the National Theater were the students. They would stand in queues for hours before the beginning of a performance and as soon as the doors were opened would rush upstairs in a body to get the best places in the gallery. The attendants who took the tickets knew most of them by name. They also got to know Martinů, in whose talents they had an unshakable belief; they were his loyal admirers right up to the days when his own operas and ballets were produced there, arguing fiercely with anyone who was not in complete accord with his ideas. Martinů also had the opportunity to hear the operas of Wagner, which were given at the New German Theater. The singer Drill Oridge, who was devoted to the Czech audiences, came to Prague at about that time to sing the roles of l'Africaine and Aïda, as well as Venus in *Tannhäuser*. Her singing made a tremendous impression on Martinů. Cold shivers ran down his spine as he listened to the unusually vibrant timbre of what seemed to him an extraordinary voice. Suddenly he felt that he understood the whole meaning of art. Immediately he began to write for voice, and later dedicated to Oridge his song-cycle with orchestral accompaniment, *Magic Nights*. He also at about that time dedicated a composition for orchestra to the Russian actress Olga Gzovska, of the Moscow Art Theater, who was idolized by the public of Prague.

He was giving so much of his time to the theater, however, as well as to reading and composition, that his violin study was beginning to suffer. As a result of this he failed in Professor Suchý's class and was transferred to that of another professor, whom he cordially disliked and with whom his marks became worse than ever. Finally he was expelled from the Conservatory for trying to eke out his tiny income by accepting an engagement for a tour with a country orchestra. There was a very strict rule that students were not permitted to play in public. Some influential citizens of Polička succeeded in having the ban lifted, however, and he returned to the Conservatory, though only for a short time; he was soon expelled again on account of some so-called carelessness. After this he enrolled as a student at the Prague School for Organ, where the famous Czech composer Leoš Janáček had studied thirty years before. This school was well known for its excellent teaching, its classes in theory being particularly good; but its main purpose was the education of future organists. Martinů, although held in great regard by his professors, simply could not get up any interest in his studies there. The truth was that schools of any kind were foreign to his nature. He lived in the clouds, completely absorbed in his own personal problems; he did not even feel it worth while to defend himself when, as once happened, he was unjustly accused of some fault committed by a colleague and punished, though innocent. Actually, as a result of his private reading and his interest in the theater, Martinů was a good deal better informed than the average student, but he had absolutely no desire to make use of his knowledge in school. Only in musical dictation was he invariably at the head of his class, for this he took down subconsciously, without any apparent effort, and therefore no preliminary work was necessary.

Naturally, under these circumstances he never completed his studies at the School for Organ; and his parents, now almost desperate over his continual failures, thought of a new possibility. They hoped that by studying as an extra-curricular student he might be able to pass the State examination in the violin, for which he would receive an officially recognized diploma entitling him to teach music in the high schools. But his first attempt on these lines was a catastrophe. He failed in every subject: violin, composition, harmony, pedagogy, and psychology. He had simply refused to study the prescribed material. A year later he made another attempt, and this time succeeded in passing the violin examination. But in the examination for composition he failed again, all because of one question; he was asked: "Can a composition start with a bare interval of a fourth?" and Martinů without hesitation replied: "Yes" — an answer that cost him his diploma.

3 : With the Czech Philharmonic, 1913–23

IN the autumn of 1913 the well-known violinist Stanislav Novák brought Martinů into the Czech Philharmonic Orchestra, seating his friend next to himself at the second stand of the first violins. Novák had been one of Martinů's closest friends ever since they were students together at the Prague Conservatory. Unluckily for Martinů, the whole of the first concert was devoted to the works of Richard Strauss, which proved to be altogether too difficult for a beginner at orchestral playing. The consequence was that at the following concert he was relegated to the third stand of the second violins, and there he remained for the rest of his stay with the Philharmonic, until 1923.

Membership in this famous orchestra brought to the young man a new circle of friends, all bound together by their common interests and very simple standard of living. At that time the Philharmonic was not the autonomous and financially secure body that it became after 1918 under the Czechoslovak Republic. It had no regular hall for rehearsals; these had to be held somewhere in the suburbs of the city. Also, during the summer it was necessary, in order to make ends meet, for the orchestra to play popular music all over the countryside. But the Philharmonic was ambitious. On the conductor's stand, permanently occupied by Vilém Zemánek, world-famous guests often appeared. Among these were Gustav Mahler, who was born in Bohemia and owed much to Prague during his early musical life, the Russian conductor Vassily Safonoff, and Felix Weingartner. The standard of the orchestra was high and its repertoire catholic. It included works by such men as Strauss, Bruckner, and Mahler as well as those of Czech composers.

At that time there were in Prague two opposing musical influences: on the one hand veneration for the national hero Smetana — whose work was often wrongly and too programmatically explained — and on the other the cult of Bruckner, Strauss, and Mahler, with their emphasis on the metaphysical and literary qualities of music rather than on form. Martinů greatly admired the brilliant technique of these last-named composers and had in particular a fondness for Mahler's songs; nevertheless he remained completely outside these various factions.[1] Their onesidedness disturbed him, and he reacted against them by concentrating on tone-color for its own sake. However, he never neglected an opportunity of hearing important new works, and when Strauss's *Elektra* and *Rosenkavalier* were given at the National Theater, he studied their structure intently, even smuggling himself into some of the rehearsals, in company with his friend Novák. But though

---

[1] At this point it may be stated that Arnold Schönberg — the "spiritual son of Bruckner, Mahler and Strauss," as Aaron Copland has correctly named him — had absolutely no influence on Martinů. The reasons are threefold: first, Martinů dislikes exasperated romanticism; secondly, he finds it impossible to express himself in the simple variation form which, according to Copland, is the principle of the "twelve-tone system"; thirdly, the Schönbergian atonality — in spite of its experimental importance — is foreign to Martinů, whose music demands much wider means of expression.

he was constantly enlarging his horizon in this way, he still remained without any definite plan for his own work.

The World War of 1914–18 brought about certain changes in Martinů's outward life, though he went on living in Prague until 1915. His great endeavor now was to evade military conscription in the Austrian Army, for his sympathies, like those of the rest of Czech youth, were openly on the side of the Western democracies. Three times he was called before a draft board, and when threatened with a fourth call abruptly left for Polička. His health had been suffering, for he had made so many efforts to simulate illness that he had finally succeeded in making himself really ill. But at his home, where he was well known as a musician, he was more successful in his efforts to keep out of the army. Not until his seventh call did it happen that a doctor who knew him well made the careless mistake of substituting his case for that of a certain very robust Mr. Březina, with the result that Martinů was drafted while Mr. Březina went free. In the end, however, matters were fortunately so arranged by Martinů's influential friends that he did not after all have to enter the army.

He now settled down to the life of a music teacher at a junior high school in Polička, also giving private lessons on the violin. He formed an ensemble of twenty violins among his third-grade pupils and arranged a good deal of music for them to play, including some compositions by Mozart and Grieg. These boys, then all about fourteen years of age, enjoyed their music sessions so much that to this day they often speak of them with enthusiasm. Gradually Martinů's financial position improved, and before long he was able to purchase a piano. He also had a certain amount of leisure for composition and wrote a number of songs, including some for children. These were commissioned by F. A. Urbánek, a music publisher in Prague, but were never printed. At this time he also composed a good deal for piano, among other things a series of pieces called *Snow*. Here in Polička his life was now calm and simple. He was in no hurry to make a success, and continued quietly, half subconsciously to collect material for a purpose that was not yet quite clear, even to himself.

Before long he became involved in a small episode of a sentimental nature. His brother František was engaged in painting the ceiling of a cloister in the small neighboring town of Želiv, and while visiting him there, Bohuslav met and fell very innocently in love with the daughter of a local family. It was the first time he had ever experienced anything of the kind, and in his youthful simplicity he looked up to her as though she were some kind of angel or saint, never realizing the amusement with which the gossips of the small town were watching the progress of this artless affair. But the interlude did not last very long, and he soon reverted to a blasé, devil-may-care attitude, his reaction expressing itself in the composition of three songs to words from Baudelaire's *Fleurs du mal*. These were written in an unexpected idiom — very modern, dissonant, even brutal.

Another work of this period was a "Small Suite" for large orchestra. In this the scoring was so intricate and there were so many *divisi* that the manuscript of this "Small Suite" grew to quite unforeseen dimensions. He also later improvised incidental music for performances given by students in the large new theater in Polička, among them Pirandello's *Six Characters in Search of an Author*. And for local amateur enthusiasts of chamber music he composed a string quartet, completely in the style of Dvořák.

After the war Martinů stayed on in Polička until 1920. There in 1918 he wrote his first really successful composition, *Czech Rhapsody* for orchestra, organ, solos, and mixed chorus. This is a patriotic work, very much in the style of Smetana — a spontaneous outpouring of the feelings of a liberated nation and the enthusiasm of its masses — completely different from

anything that Martinů had done up to that time. His feeling
for people in the mass plays an important part in his work and
is clearly shown in his later compositions *Half-Time*, *La
Bagarre*, *La Rhapsodie*, and *Field Mass*, as well as, to some
extent, in the Double Concerto. In the *Czech Rhapsody* he
makes use of an old Czech chorale, *St. Wenceslaus*, and also
one of the psalms which had remained in his memory from
the days of his occasional visits to play the organ in the
Protestant church of near-by Borová, the church which used
to be attended by the family of Thomas Garrigue Masaryk.
The *Czech Rhapsody* was given its first performance in 1919,
by the Philharmonic Orchestra in Prague, under L. V. Čelanský; and at a subsequent performance President Masaryk was
present in the audience.

In 1920 Martinů returned to Prague and took his old place
among the second violins of the Czech Philharmonic Orchestra, which had in the meanwhile been reorganized on a sounder
financial basis, with Václav Talich as musical director. Arduous rehearsals were held every day, and the organization was
beginning again to reach a high standard. Its repertoire was
larger and more complete than previously and now included
most of the great works of Beethoven, Brahms, and Dvořák.
For Martinů, however, the most important acquisition of this
new library was the modern French music, which he eagerly
studied. In addition to Debussy, some of whose lesser compositions he had already played in the orchestra in 1914, he now
grew familiar with Ravel, Dukas, and Roussel; and for the
first time he made the acquaintance of Igor Stravinsky's music,
which was introduced to the Prague public in interpretations
that were perfect to the last detail.

During this period of his life (1920–3) Martinů began to
find himself almost a solitary figure in an environment where
content was considered more important than form. For him
organic unity — the complete realization of an idea, the perfect   ·

16

conformity of content and expression — in short, form rather than formalism — was the main problem. These were difficult times for him, because often his surroundings induced in him a feeling that he was possibly mistaken and might be following the wrong path. His own ideas were still vague and instinctive, and his efforts to express himself were often handicapped by a lack of technical knowledge. All the same, he could not rid himself of the conviction that there was something basically false in the current philosophical and ideological interpretation of music in the German style. He soon realized that unfortunately a musical trend is not determined so much by musicians as by critics and musicologists. But the pioneer work of Talich gradually resolved his secret doubts, and Debussy became to him the greatest revelation of this period. Latin ideas in matters of art find sympathetic understanding among Czech musicians, as well as with painters and writers; so even in this respect Martinů is a true son of his country, which, though it stands at the cross-roads of eastern and western Europe, consciously accepts Western culture. The only exception to this is in the influence of folk music.

Martinů made his debut in 1922 at the Prague National Theater, with his ballet *Istar,* based on the Oriental story of Astarte, Goddess of Spring. Choreographically the ballet was magnificently presented by Jelizaveta Nikolska, who herself danced the title role; and the work made an excellent impression as to both sound and structure. This was a sad time for the composer, however, who just at that moment received the news that his father had died in Polička. Another work, *Vanishing Midnight,* from his Three Symphonic Poems, was also produced about that time by the Philharmonic Orchestra. His First String Quartet — completely under the influence of Debussy — dates back to the same period. It is well written, full of color, and fairly sound in structure — the work of a real composer in spite of its obvious defects. Martinů's desk was

17

filled with manuscripts of all kinds, some of them songs set to Chinese and other exotic words. But these were somewhat contemptuously referred to as "French" by the Prague critics, implying a certain inferiority in comparison with the more profound German style of music then in vogue. This classification as "French" tagged Martinů for a long time and was the source of many of his spiritual struggles, for at heart he was completely a Czech.

In 1922, at the suggestion of Josef Suk, Martinů again entered the Prague Conservatory. This time the circumstances were quite different. The institution had undergone considerable change under the free Republic, and many new personalities were now on the professorial staff. Among these was Josef Suk, second violin of the famous Bohemian Quartet, who was in charge of a master class in composition. He gave lectures to his five most advanced pupils, and told them a great deal about the work of his father-in-law, Antonín Dvořák. Suk heartily welcomed Martinů to these classes, and their mutual relations were always pleasant. But, as before, Martinů found it impossible to work under school conditions. He often said that he liked Suk very much, but Martinů was, as the Czechs put it, a "free bird" and could really be influenced by no one. In nearly a year's attendance at the Conservatory he did not even produce a piano sketch for the orchestral overture which was a prescribed task for the students. And before the year was up he had again left the school.

One of the advantages of membership in the Czech Philharmonic was the traveling involved during its visits to foreign countries. To Martinů, with his innately cosmopolitan outlook, these tours contributed a great deal. As far back as 1919 he had at his own request accompanied the orchestra of the National Theater, under the conductorship of Karel Kovařovič, on a concert tour which included Geneva, Paris, and London. Later, with the Czech Philharmonic, he went on an extensive visit to Italy, to which in subsequent years he often returned on vacation. He was much influenced by London and Paris; and Italian light-heartedness and lack of inhibition gave him a peculiar feeling of affinity. These sporadic trips abroad could not but affect his future and help him to a gradual realization of his aims. Paris in particular held a special allure for him. And one day in Prague, while playing Roussel's symphonic piece *Poème de la forêt*, he suddenly realized where his loyalties lay. At once his inner struggles came to an end, and he knew that he must go to Paris. By a lucky coincidence he was at that moment offered a modest State grant, just enough to keep him for three months. So in September 1923 he left Prague for Paris, still oppressed by various problems and full of contradictions. At the time the venture seemed like a small excursion, but actually it turned out to be one of the most important decisions of Martinů's life; for he remained in Paris for seventeen years, leaving only after the fall of France in 1940. He was thirty-three years old when he arrived there, and all his works up to that time were significant chiefly for what they seemed to foreshadow.

4 : In Paris: Adaptation and Absorption

MARTINŮ was utterly lost in his new environment. He tried vainly to find a room on the boulevard Saint-Michel, and after wandering about for a long time, suitcase in hand, finally decided to put up in the rue aux Ours, near les Halles, the great market of Paris. His hotel, a small place in the commercial section, proved to be quite impossible, and he soon moved to another on the rue des Dames in Montmartre. As soon as he was settled he looked up Albert Roussel, who had some time before retired from official musical life, though still very active in music, and Martinů began to take lessons from him. Owing to their difference of nationality they found it somewhat difficult to communicate with each other; and Martinů's inadequate knowledge of French served only to increase his natural timidity. But their common language was music, and it was not long before their relationship became one of friendly mutual admiration. Martinů, usually half an hour late, would be received by the kind, reserved man, together with his inseparable cat. And though at first no new results appeared from these lessons, Martinů gradually began to feel that he was on the right road at last. Roussel was able to teach him much in the way of Gallic lightness and elegance. All the same, in the opinion of the French composer Martinů's style was, and always would remain, essentially Czech in character. Being himself somewhat lacking in vitality, Roussel particularly liked the healthy, virile tone of Martinů's work. And the younger man, on his side, felt a great esteem for Roussel's symphonies, though his favorite always remained the simple, charming ballet *Le Festin d'Araignée*.

Paris enchanted Martinů. At night, instead of sleeping, he wandered all over the city, completely fascinated by the bright lights and the gay night life of the boulevards. Pre-eminently an observer ever since his days in the Polička tower, he loved to stroll by himself along the quais of the Seine, constantly stopping to pore over the contents of the book-stalls. The *bouquinistes* got to know him well, for every afternoon between the hours of three and five he might be seen taking the long walks that were such an important feature of his life in the capital. Martinů once calculated that in ten years of these promenades he must have spent exactly a year on the quais of the Seine.

Here, on "the quais of optimism," as Martinů called the quais of the Seine, he found, in his hours of rest, *Špaliček* and many of his other inspirations.[1] Later, when he had more money, there was hardly a day when he did not acquire some new treasure for his rapidly growing library. Instinctively he responded to the accumulated culture and tradition of Paris. This new life seemed to be the answer to all his questions. The very air breathed liberty. Suddenly Martinů felt himself free.

Now began a period, such as has occurred several times during his life, when he rested and lay fallow. During these times he wrote practically nothing — he just read, analyzed the scores of the old masters, and observed life. Subconsciously he was slowly maturing for further composition. Owing to lack of money he could not afford to rent a piano; and his extremely meager knowledge of the French language made contact with people well-nigh impossible. The well-known Czech painter Jan Zrzavý, who hailed from the same part of the country as Martinů, was almost his only companion in those days.

Paris in the 1920's was the center not only of modern music but of modern painting and literature. Composers, painters, and poets from all over the world used to meet in the Montparnasse quarter and discuss the future of art. At that time there was a strong reaction against the romantic style, and a good deal of confusion of ideas existed. Those were the days of the famous Russian Ballet of Diaghilev, featuring works by Stravinsky and the "Groupe des Six." Martinů found many of these surprising and disturbing. Some, of more typically Parisian character, seemed to him lacking in seriousness and were in complete contradiction to his opinions on art and the mission of the artist. He disliked the current trend for novelty at any price. In short, many ideas of this *avantgardiste* period were completely unacceptable to him; and, with few exceptions (the music of Honegger, for example), he re-

---

[1] See Martinů's article *"Pařížská Nábřeží"* in *New Yorské Listy*, October 28, 1943.

mained unconvinced by the new French music that he heard. On the other hand, he was strongly influenced by Stravinsky, in whose works he found the answer to many of his questions regarding new methods of technique.

Martinů's reaction to the impacts of his new environment appeared only gradually. His powers of adaptation, never very great, were not equal to the strain, which was accentuated by his difficult living-conditions. He began to realize that under the great French tradition much hard work would be necessary before he could reach his goal. Distrusting current polyphony, he composed very little, and then only in his former harmonic style. He gave none of his works to the public and many he destroyed. His Paris was at that time a small room in the rue Delambre in Montparnasse; [2] here he read a great deal and kept in close contact with those of the modern French painters who were concerned more with Poussin and Chardin than with cubism, and who, like himself, were going through an intense spiritual struggle under the hard conditions of modern life. And at each step he was confronted with the living influence of the great French artists of the past. This was a new period of absorption.

In Paris, Martinů found the quiet so necessary for his work, and that was the main reason why he remained there for seventeen years. In Paris a man can isolate himself more than anywhere else. Many years ago, when he visited Paris, František Langer, well-known Czech playwright, sought avidly the reasons why this Czech composer lived and composed in Paris and not in Prague. He was surprised when Martinů did not speak of the material and spiritual advantages of his voluntary exile in the world's cultural metropolis, but praised instead the peace and quiet, and the possibilities of complete isolation which Paris afforded for his work.

---

[2] After leaving Montmartre Martinů moved several times into the apartments of friends, and at one time lived in Jan Masaryk's apartment in the rue Jasmin.

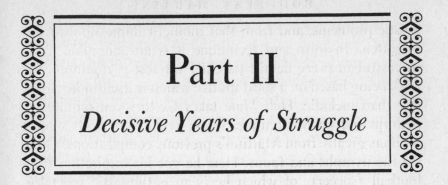

Part II
Decisive Years of Struggle

5 : Half-Time

MARTINŮ'S period of silent receptivity, which lasted for a year and a half, was suddenly interrupted by the orchestral work *Half-Time*, written in Polička during his summer vacation of 1925. This was first produced by the Czech Philharmonic under Václav Talich and given its second performance at the Festival for Contemporary Music, which happened that year to be held in Prague. At the first performance public opinion was sharply divided, some of the audience responding with great enthusiasm while in others the piece roused an equally strong aversion. So remarkable was its effect upon the listeners that one musician — later conductor of the National Theater Orchestra — showed his disapproval by actually fighting with his bare fists a group of Martinů's admirers who had assembled in force to cheer the performance. This incident naturally attracted a good deal of attention and heightened the contentious effect of the work.[1]

Half-Time is totally different from any of Martinů's previous music, and shows unmistakably the influence of Stravinsky. In its composition he seems to have solved many of his

---

[1] This conductor, however, later gave the first performance of Martinů's opera *The Miracle of Our Lady* at the National Theater in Prague.

artistic problems, and from that moment impressionism was forgotten. In form and technique it is an admirable work, successful in every detail. Its chief interest is rhythmic, the work being based on a short motive which is itself more rhythmic than melodic. *Half-Time* takes six to seven minutes to perform and was written in a single week. Even in its subject it differs greatly from Martinů's previous compositions. Gone are the nymphs and fauns. Here he got his inspiration from football (soccer), of which he is an enthusiastic spectator. This game is very popular in Czechoslovakia, which from 1919 to 1923 held the world championship. *Half-Time* is marked fortissimo throughout, except for some passages of strongly Czech character on the trumpets, and is conceived chiefly in terms of the brass instruments. The strings merely mark the rhythm. It gives the listener the impression of a motor that stops at exactly the right moment. This psychological understanding of the point at which the end of a composition should be reached is one of Martinů's most important gifts. If this piece had been even a few bars longer, there might have been some risk of monotony. *Half-Time* contains in embryo many features of Martinů's future work. Its rhythm is irregular, free from the tyranny of the bar-line. It is atonal in character and brutal in sound. The piano, which in Martinů's orchestral works plays a prominent role both for its tone-color and for its percussive quality, is here used as an instrument of the orchestra. In short, the work was a product of the times, in which rhythmic and dynamic elements were a feature, as in Honegger's *Pacific 231*, written in 1923 and first performed in 1924. Martinů had never heard Honegger's composition when he wrote *Half-Time*, though naturally he was acquainted with Stravinsky's *Le Sacre du printemps*.

Half-Time [2] is a typical example of a process which appeared

---

[2] The MS. of this work was lost in Paris and is not accessible in America. A copy exists somewhere in Europe.

from time to time during the course of Martinů's creative work. Apparently unpremeditated, a composition would suddenly crystallize, new in form and technique and not appearing to fit logically into the expected development of his style. These deviations from his normal course are always sudden, harsh, and violent. The Trio for violin, cello, and piano, the *Inventions* for orchestra, the Double Concerto, the First Cello Sonata, and in certain respects the opera *Juliette* are similar instances. These "unexpected" compositions are often more nearly perfect than those more obviously expected in his development. He does not as a rule, however, continue immediately upon his newly discovered path. The effects of these "unexpected" works are usually not evident until later, often after a series of compositions in an earlier manner.

Thus the hard impact of *Half-Time* is not to be found in either *La Bagarre* or *Rhapsody*, both for large orchestra, which were written shortly after. Though in these rhythmic interest is paramount their mood is more lyrical, and Martinů's sense of form and order is always evident. *La Bagarre (Tumult)* is best explained by the notes Martinů prepared for the program of the Boston Symphony Orchestra, which introduced his music to America by giving the première of this work on November 18 and 19, 1927, in Boston, under Serge Koussevitzky, also performing it in Providence, Rhode Island, and New York during the same season. Martinů writes:

"La Bagarre" is charged with an atmosphere of movement, dash, tumult, obstruction. It is a movement in grand mass, in uncontrollable, violent rush. I dedicate the composition to the memory of Lindbergh landing at Bourget, which responds to my imagination, and expresses clearly its aim and evolution. In "Half-Time," [3] [which is a] symphonic rondo, 2–2, I have portrayed the tension of spectators at a game of football. "Bagarre" is, properly speaking, an analogous subject, but multi-

[3] The word "Half-Time" was accidentally omitted in the Boston Symphony program.

plied, transported to the street. It's a boulevard, a stadium, a mass, a quantity which is in delirium, clothed as a single body. It's a chaos, ruled by all the sentiments of enthusiasm, struggle, joy, sadness, wonder. It's a chaos governed by a common feeling, an invisible bond, which pushes everything forward, which moulds numerous masses into a single element full of unexpected, uncontrollable events. It is grandly contrapuntal. All interests, great and small, disappear as secondary themes, and are fused at the same time in a new composition of movement, in a new expression of force, in a new form of powerful, unconquerable human mass. But "La Bagarre" is not descriptive music. It is determined according to the laws of composition; it has its chief theme — as the human crowd has its theme of enthusiasm — which directs the movement. "La Bagarre," properly speaking, is a triptych, in which the intermediate phrase, usually free, is replaced (apparently by a more melodious movement) by a quicker tempo than that of the first and the third, ending in a violent, presto coda.

In the upper right-hand corner of the score, as noted by the critic A. H. M.[4] in the Boston *Transcript* of November 17, 1927, are scribbled in pencil the words: "En souvenir de Lindbergh, à Le Bourget" ("In memory of the landing of Lindbergh at Le Bourget"). *La Bagarre* was not composed, A. H. M. continues, to celebrate Lindbergh's achievement, as was James P. Dunn's composition *We*. For the last page of the score bears the words: "Paris, Mai, 1926 B. Martinů," in ink visibly of the same age as the ink of the rest of the page. Consequently the pencil notation at the beginning of the score is an afterthought.

La Bagarre is certainly not a description of the landing at Le Bourget, with its mechanical sounds and incidents. It is, as Alfred H. Mayer very pertinently pointed out:

an extended development of two themes — both interesting and decidedly musical rather than cerebral — as beautifully contrasted as ever were themes in an orthodox sonata-form. The first theme (in C-minor) played by the strings, consists of four measures of rapid eighth notes staccato. It is a theme entirely typical of the mechanistic age in

[4] Alfred H. Mayer, now head of the Music Department of Boston University.

music, a theme the propulsive hardness of whose rhythm would not have presented itself to the imagination of a composer a decade ago. Shortly the second theme enters. The tonality has changed to C-major. The theme — again of four measures and again for strings — is a flowing and entirely ingratiating cantabile. Both are repeated, exactly as though one were dealing with a sonata-exposition. Development begins, which means that the tumult grows. Persistent, obstinate rhythms inject their incisive mood. There are sharp punctuations (brass) in even accented quarter notes. Now and again the tumult subsides. During one such lull three solo violins sing the cantabile theme in fifths and thirds, or common major chords. The prevailing eighth-note rhythm gives way to more rapid triplet schemes. Intoxicating, swirling, figures are superimposed upon rhythms and harmonies that remind one of nothing so much as the ticking of a huge clock.[5] The two main themes are by no means lost in the melée, and subsidiary thematic fragments also play their part. Catastrophic chords break in here and there. The whole ends in a blaze of fury. The orchestration of "La Bagarre" is that of the modern full orchestra with complete battery of percussion including piano. The score is not particularly chromatic but the clashing of tonalities is frequent.

According to Leslie A. Sloper of the *Christian Science Monitor* (November 19, 1927), *La Bagarre* had "the greatest popular success that has been won at Symphony Hall by a novelty for a long time. Its success was by no means entirely due to its topical interest. It has definite musical values." "Seldom has an unfamiliar composition, one by an unknown composer, been so enthusiastically welcomed in Symphony Hall; it is fresh, virile music, the ecstatic expression of strength, power, dominance," said the Boston *Herald* of the same date. According to the Boston *Post* (same date), "It is more melodic in character, more orderly in construction, less dissonant and dynamically violent than any other modernist piece. Martinů's tumult is surprisingly tame, precise and circumspect."

[5] See p. 4 for the ticking of the huge tower clock in Martinů's birthplace, Polička.

This is the moment to say one or two words about the conductors who recognized his talent and helped Martinů. There are several: Václav Talich, Paul Sacher, Ernest Ansermet, Charles Munch, and Serge Koussevitzky; but of these the last is unquestionably one of the most important. Speaking to newspapermen before the performance of *La Bagarre*, which was Martinů's first work to be played in the United States, Dr. Koussevitzky revealed how he discovered Martinů's talent.[6] In Paris a very young-looking man approached him with the request that he examine a score. The conductor judged the youth to be over twenty-two (actually Martinů then was thirty-six). The first page of the manuscript gave the impression of mastery. Koussevitzky looked farther, became interested, and completed this first reading of the score with enthusiasm.

Thus Koussevitzky discovered Martinů for America. His interest in the work of this Czech composer has continually grown, as is evident from the number of premières of Martinů's works that he has conducted, as well as by the fact that he later commissioned the First Symphony.

The *Rhapsody* bears the date: Paris, May 14, 1928 — exactly two years after *La Bagarre*. Martinů wrote it to celebrate the presentation of the Czechoslovak flag to the First Czechoslovak Regiment, at Darney, France, on June 30, 1918 — the first grand symbolic episode in the history of independent Czechoslovakia. The *Rhapsody* has many points of resemblance with *La Bagarre*. It is a great symphonic march, with an important solo for English horn in the middle. The composer himself hesitated for some time over the title of this work. At first he had in mind a symphony of military character; and to a certain extent it is possible to look upon this composition as a symphony in three movements without a break. But when it was first given in Boston, he wrote that he would prefer to speak of it as "a grand march with a melodic

---

6 See Boston *Transcript*, November 17, 1927.

contrast," and then decided to call it *La Symphonie*. The definite article *La* in the title is without doubt significant, for *La Symphonie* is not what is usually understood by a symphony. Perhaps Martinů himself gave the best answer to this question — which was much discussed by the critics on the occasion of the Boston performance — by calling another symphony that he composed in America fourteen years later his "First Symphony." *La Symphonie* was also played in Paris by the Orchestre Straram in 1929 under the title *Allegro symphonique*. In Prague, conducted by Ernest Ansermet, it was finally designated *Rhapsody*.

Half-Time, *La Bagarre*, and *La Symphonie* brought international recognition to Martinů. But his everyday life did not change. He went on living in real poverty in his small room in Montparnasse, which was just large enough to hold a bed, a piano, a writing-table, and a small stove. This last was a most important part of his furniture, for he cooked all his own meals, which usually consisted of the cheapest fish he could buy. To save himself time and trouble he often prepared enough to last for several days. A Czech cartoonist once made a caricature in which Martinů is shown holding a piano between his long thin legs while simultaneously cooking and composing. In this room he kept his books and scores — on shelves, on chairs, on the bed, on the piano, everywhere. Slowly he was accumulating all that has been contributed by the great minds of the world. Among his scores was music that will never grow old — Bach, Mozart, Palestrina, Corelli, Orlando di Lasso. He himself was still the same shy, modest, youthful-looking man who never sought opportunities or fame. As though from a tower — in this case his small, poor room — he kept up a detached observation of the prosperous Paris of post-war years. Already he had a small but devoted circle of friends. Every night they met in the Café du Dôme in Montparnasse, a rendezvous for a little group of musicians, mostly foreigners, just as he was. There was Marcel Mihalovici, who had come from Bucharest for two weeks, and to this day still lives in France; Tibor Harsanyi, Hungarian pianist and composer; and Conrad Beck, the Swiss composer. These three men shared a great admiration for Martinů, and soon a "Groupe des Quatre" was formed, in which all four helped each other as though they were brothers, and by their discussions and exchange of manuscripts often arrived at results which are not without value in the history of modern music.

But Martinů was still at the very beginning of his struggle for an expression of his own. Paris and France had widened his horizon, confirmed his desire for order and purity of expression, and strengthened his aversion to cheap sensation. He feels with Charles Péguy that "there exist passions which can be as flat as a billiard table, while temperance and reasonableness can be as full and heavy as ripe grapes." More and more strongly he realized that he was not a Frenchman but a Czech — even though the news was reaching him that in his homeland, where *Half-Time* was just beginning to be known, it was dubbed "French."

6 : Chamber Music

AFTER *Half-Time*, *La Bagarre*, and *Rhapsody* Martinů practically abandoned the large orchestra and for several years devoted himself to chamber music and music for chamber orchestra. This he continued right up to the time of the composition of his First Symphony in the United States in 1942. The only exceptions were the opera *Juliette*, a reorchestration of his ballet *Špaliček*, and the Cello Concerto. Actually he was returning to chamber music after a break of two years, for in 1926 he had written his Second String Quartet. This work was given its première in Berlin in 1927 in an excellent performance by the Novák-Frank Quartet, and soon after was played in all the musical centers of Europe, as well as in America. It is similar to *Half-Time* in that it lays the foundation of a new style in Martinů's chamber music, just as *Half-Time* did in his orchestral work. Somewhat feverish in feeling and overfull of material, it is a dynamic, even eruptive work, written with an excellent understanding of quartet technique. The original version was composed in Paris. Unfortunately the first movement, much influenced by Stravinsky, did not please the cellist Frank, for whose quartet it was written. So Martinů took the manuscript along with him on a vacation in Polička, and there rewrote it in the form in which it is now published in the Universal Edition, Vienna. The trouble was that then the first two movements were better than the third. He therefore again set to work and produced a new third movement, actually writing it in the National Café in Prague, because the Novák-Frank organization was on the point of leaving for a concert tour and wanted to take it with them. This work was followed by the String Quintet and the Sextet for strings — both more nearly perfect in form — which are to some extent derived from this quartet, being conceived in the same manner, which is pure Martinů and free from outside influence; for Martinů in rewriting the greater part of the composition had finally found his personal expression.

It was also for Novák and Frank that he wrote his Duo for violin and cello, which has been more widely performed all the world over than any of his other works. It even exists in a recorded version — a most unusual occurrence with Martinů's music. In its two movements (Preludium and Rondo) the technical possibilities of the instruments are exploited to the fullest extent, and there are two brilliant cadenzas.

While living in his garret in the rue de Delambre, Martinů

began gradually to return to the fundamentals of music as well
as to himself. Ever since the beginning of his work at composition — ten years before in Prague — he had felt that the
development of harmony and its culmination in the nineteenth century were in contradiction to his aims and temperament. Already in his two books of piano pieces, *Puppets*
(1908–9) he had shown himself in disagreement with current
sentimental trends. Exaggerated sentiment and the apotheosis
of the composer's personality, with its egotistical interest in
his own sensations, fantasies, and pleasures rather than in
the rest of the world, were repugnant to him. He had absolutely no desire further to complicate harmony, in the sense
in which it was then understood. Even the counterpoint of
Bach did not entirely satisfy his strenuous search. He was more
interested in the primitive, naïve counterpoint of the old
Flemish masters, in the Masses of Palestrina, in Josquin des
Près, Orlando di Lasso, and Guillaume Dufay, one of the first
composers to introduce the use of popular songs into church
music — in all who by simple means attained an emotional
effect in the beauty of pure sound. (He cared less for Monte-
verdi, in whose work a more modern sense of harmony becomes evident.) Rather than in vertical harmony Martinů is
interested in the chords arrived at by a free horizontal conduct
of voices. Long before the war the English Singers, who often
appeared before the Czech Chamber Music Society[1] in
Prague, had been a great revelation to him. At that time he
could not afford to buy the expensive English edition of the
madrigals they sang; only later was he able to spare two hundred francs in order to secure a few books of them. Consequently he became acquainted with the madrigals only

---

[1] This society, the largest chamber-music organization in the world, was
founded in the 1890's by sponsors of the Bohemian String Quartet. In 1914 it had
over 4,000 subscribers. Membership was inherited from generation to generation
and it was practically impossible to become a new subscriber. Its concerts were
held in two subscription series in the Smetana Hall in Prague.

through listening to them. But they confirmed his own theories and he realized to what an extent the harmonic structure dominating the nineteenth century has hampered individual parts and bound them together without giving them their rightful freedom. And now Paris — where Guillaume de Machaut introduced free part-writing (as in his Mass for the Coronation of Charles V) — was the right place for Martinů in his struggle towards a new polyphony. The whole period, culminating in Debussy, was a critical one. Everything was beginning to disintegrate and there seemed to be no way out. A composer might at that time write in the classical or romantic style, continue with impressionism, or dabble in dadaism. In not one of these schools could Martinů drop anchor with conviction. Naturally, every serious composer of that time contributed something, but only in exceptional cases was it in the real interest of music.

Martinů's work necessarily fell at this time into forms in which he was able to express his ideas naturally. Consequently he wrote chiefly chamber music and compositions for chamber orchestra during the year 1930. Being anxious to make some money, he was working for several music publishers, among them A. Leduc, Deiss, and La Sirène Musicale of Paris, as well as Schott and Sons of Mainz, who published about a dozen of his compositions during 1930 and 1931.

He had furnished a small flat in rue Mandar, in the commercial section of Paris; and in 1931 he married Charlotte Quennehen, a young Frenchwoman from Picardy, whom he had known for several years. She was a simple, courageous girl who earned her living as a couturière, and who also had known hardship in her life. The marriage, in addition to providing the composer with a home, brought about a substantial change in his existence; for he was undoubtedly influenced by the realistic qualities inherent in the French nature. His wife, never very strong, was ill at about that time; and

33

Martinů, in his desire to give her every care, now worked doubly hard.

During 1930 and 1931 he produced a great number of works. One of these, the First Violin Sonata, is in jazz idiom.[2] More characteristic of him are the Third String Quartet and the Second Violin Sonata, which are both written in a clear, simple style. The quartet is a merry work of Czech character, delicately brittle in sound, as though made of porcelain — a complete contrast to the Second String Quartet. Among his compositions of that time are also three books of rhythmic studies (*Études rhythmiques*) for violin and cello, which, though written for the purpose of helping students to adapt themselves to the playing of modern music, actually prepared the soil for his own new works. In these studies the bowing technique is particularly interesting. More important from the point of view of his future development are Five Short Pieces for violin and piano, which clearly foreshadow one of Martinů's greatest chamber works, the Trio for piano, violin, and cello.

In examining this Trio — which he composed in one breath, as it were, between May 20 and May 30, 1930 — we notice his use of a new, direct polyphony. The composer himself was astounded by the fluency of the creative impulse that brought this work into being, and in typical Martinů manner said to me: "I don't know how I came to write it; suddenly, as though I acquired a different hand, I wrote something entirely new." Thus we see that although he is a diligent student of musical æsthetics and a gifted theorist there are some secrets of his creative process which even he does not understand. This powerful work represents a turning-point in his development. His ideas suddenly dovetailed into a long-sought pattern, creating

---

[2] The first of Martinů's compositions in this style is the Suite from his ballet *Revue de cuisine* (*Kitchen Review*). He also used jazz in his opera *Suburban Theater*.

a more uniform work than before, in which the phrases are independent of the bar-line and all three instruments are given an extreme polyphonic freedom. This is impersonal music, modern in the best sense of the word; perhaps the finest compliment it ever received was from a sculptor who said that it is built in marble.

The example which follows shows the three initial bars of the first movement (Allegro moderato):

This is a completely different technique from anything ever used by Martinů before. There is no main theme and development, but a number of small "cells" (to use his own expression) with which he plays. The effect of this new technique is most successful, although it cannot be defined.

The second movement (Adagio) is a free polyphony reminiscent of Corelli.

Another example, taken from the fourth movement (Allegro moderato), is characteristic of the harmonic polyphony which Martinů later developed in his orchestral works:

Ironically, the première of the Trio was far from successful. It had been commissioned by the Trio Belge, which went to Paris in order to play it there. But the performance was a catastrophe. Martinů — who never looks very far for the cause of a failure, and is under no great illusion regarding his own work — thought that the composition rather than the performance was to blame. The work was given again about two years later, however, by the Triton, a society for contemporary music in Paris, of which Pierre-Octave Ferroud, a warm admirer of Martinů's work, was the moving spirit; and on this occasion it was excellently played by the Trio Hongrois, with the result that, to Martinů's surprise and pleasure, the critics and most of the public acclaimed it with enthusiasm. After this it was played all over Europe (including a performance in the house of Nadia Boulanger, who has always followed Martinů's career with unusual interest); and no matter what other works were given at the same time the Trio always proved to be the climax of the program.

At about this period Martinů's String Sextet earned a particular honor; it won the Elizabeth Sprague Coolidge Prize for 1932 [3] in America, being chosen from 145 works submitted from all over the world.[4] "It is a real string sextet," wrote Olin Downes,[5] "and not a quartet with two extra instruments. The American audience received Martinů's work with a rare enthusiasm for its strength, freshness and swing, uncommon vitality, musical interest, rare distinction and real creative power."

I had occasion to hear the Sextet in company with Albert Roussel, at a private concert given by Mrs. Coolidge at the Majestic Hôtel in Paris. Pride and enthusiasm glowed in the eyes of Martinů's former teacher, who was particularly impressed by the vitality of the work.

The String Quintet, the manuscript of which is in the Library of Congress in Washington, became very popular in the United States. It was played for the first time at one of the Coolidge Chamber Music Festivals in Pittsfield, Massachusetts. The first movement is tumultuous, restless, almost overfull of material, and written in a peculiarly sweeping manner. An elegiac melody of Czech character, played by the violas, dominates the second movement (Adagio); and the last movement (Allegretto) is conceived in a vein of dashing impetuosity. Fifteen years later, when it was played in Washington by the Britt String Ensemble, the Quintet was found to have lost none of its originality and power.

[3] The jury on this occasion was composed of Olin Downes, John Alden Carpenter, Louis Persinger, Carl Engel, and Serge Koussevitzky. The Coolidge Prize was $1,000 given by the Library of Congress under the provisions of the Elizabeth Sprague Coolidge Foundation.

[4] An incident very typical of Martinů occurred in connection with the Coolidge Prize. The telegram from America informing him that he had been awarded the prize, and that the sum of $1,000 in francs had been deposited in his name in a certain Paris bank, lay on his table for ten days. Its contents had been explained to him, but he thought it was a practical joke played by his friends in Montparnasse. Finally the violinist Samuel Dushkin managed to convince him that the telegram was real. The news was all the more welcome because Martinů's wife was at that time seriously ill with pneumonia and had to be sent to a hospital. He had been much worried about financial matters in connection with this, although Dushkin had generously helped in making the necessary arrangements.

[5] *New York Times*, April 25, 1933.

7 : The Path to the Concerto Grosso

MARTINŮ had been interested for some years in the concerto-grosso form, and had used it in 1931 in his String Quartet with orchestra. The works of Corelli, considered to be the founder of this style, astonished Martinů by their simplicity of structure and spiritual vivacity. He was already a great admirer of the Brandenburg Concertos in those days, and now he closely studied Corelli's Concerti Grossi and Sonate da Camera, which had influenced both Bach and Handel. Though he did not draw direct inspiration from these, he was conscious of a very strong response, largely due to his constant struggle against the exaggerated richness and emotion of harmonic music. The sonata form, so ideal for subjective expression, the two contrasting themes of which have been interpreted by romanticists as two worlds at war with each other, did not satisfy Martinů's search for a pure musical level. He was not concerned with neo-classical music or with pastiches of the old masters; what he was looking for was a vehicle for his own truly modern expression. For some years he had been making plans for a series of what might be described as "Prague concertos"; and it was only natural that the concerto-grosso form, with its possibilities for a free treatment of part-writing and polyphony, should attract him. To this day he applies it even to a symphony. As he had long been interested in vocal forms, such as madrigals, motets, and folk-songs, his attitude can be defined in the same words as those in which Sir Donald Tovey speaks about Bach: "Bach's chief concerto form is in every particular derived from the typical vocal aria, at least as regards the first movement." [1] Tovey further

---

[1] *Essays in Musical Analysis*, Vol. III, "Concertos." Oxford University Press.

states that Bach's concerto forms, with the exception of those of dramatic nature, are completely identical with his vocal forms. In any case it was inevitable that Martinů should finally arrive at a musical expression so well able to satisfy his desire for simplicity, clarity, and precision.

As so often in his life, it was by sheer coincidence that he finally stabilized his ideas on the subject. In 1931 a group of friends met in a small café in Montparnasse, after a concert given by the Pro Arte Quartet, and the artists took the occasion to ask Martinů to write a quartet with orchestral accompaniment. Immediately he realized the close relation between such a form and the tutti and solos of the concerto grosso. The idea attracted him, and the next morning he promptly set to work. Many new technical ideas and problems of sonority were involved in the outline of his plans. In the first movement (Allegro vivo, 2–2) he made use of the form, customary in the concerto grosso, of a continuous development, with variations; the usual second subject is absent, the entire movement being based on one motive, which is used in both solos and tutti. The second movement (Adagio, 4–4) is also free in conception and includes many technically important solos for the quartet. Only in the last movement (Tempo moderato, 2–4) does Martinů return to a well-known form — the Rondo.

The Pro Arte produced this interesting work in London, Brussels, Vienna, and elsewhere. While on tour in the United States they played it on April 9, 1936 with the New York Philharmonic Orchestra under Hans Lange and in Los Angeles with Pierre Monteux. The first American performance was given in 1932 by Serge Koussevitzky with the Boston Symphony Orchestra and a string quartet composed of the leaders of the various string sections. It was also recently played (1942) in Carnegie Hall by the WQXR Quartet and the National Orchestral Association, conducted by Leon Barzin. This concert offered an interesting opportunity for comparison with

Martinů's later works — the Concerto Grosso of 1938 in particular — and well illustrated his development through the intervening years.

An analogy might be made between the Quartet with orchestra and the Concertino for piano trio and orchestra,[2] written two years later; also with the Concerto for harpsichord and chamber orchestra of 1935. In the interval Martinů produced a whole series of concertos for solo instruments with orchestra, all written for special soloists. Important among them is the Second Piano Concerto, dedicated to Germaine Leroux, often performed in Europe and America.[3] In the case of the Concerto for cello and chamber orchestra the artist was Gaspar Cassadò. This work is written in a style bordering on rhythmic and harmonic license even bolder than that of *Half-Time*, and has many similarities with the Trio for violin, cello, and piano composed at about the same time. Though full of a driving tension, it does not compare with the freedom later reached by Martinů in, for example, his *Tre Ricercari*. The Cello Concerto exists in two versions: it was originally written in concerto-grosso style with chamber orchestra and was performed in Paris with extraordinary success by Pierre Fournier with the Paris Philharmonic under Charles Munch; but Martinů, while still in France in 1939, made a second version for large orchestra. A more expressive composition of this period is the Partita (Suite I). The composer heard this work for the first time in New York,[4] eleven years after writing it, and although then able to look upon it quite impersonally, was agreeably surprised by its concise and solid structure. *Serenade*, of the same year, is of a distinctly more lyrical nature.

---

[2] Martinů completely forgot this composition and was much surprised when Tibor Harsanyi performed it for the Triton in Paris in 1936.

[3] Martinů reorchestrated this Concerto in New York, in January 1944.

[4] Performed by Alfred Wallenstein's Sinfonietta on the New York radio station WOR, in 1942.

The *Inventions* for orchestra (strings, with two brass and two woodwinds) differs greatly from Martinů's prevailing style of that period. This composition — which "decidedly carried off the laurels" [5] at the International Music Festival of Venice in 1934, for which it was specially written — concentrates chiefly on tone-color. Not in the impressionistic style, it is to a certain extent polyphonic, in some ways foreshadowing the coming opera *Juliette*. Just as *Half-Time* might be looked upon as a canvas painted with broad, elemental strokes of the brush, *Inventions* can be compared to a mosaic of tiny fragments skillfully assembled into a beautiful design. It contains nothing that remotely resembles a conventional melody or theme; and apart from the name it has nothing in common with the *Inventions* of Bach, except possibly with the free counterpoint of Bach's F-minor three-part Invention. Martinů's work is in three sections, of which the first and third are fast, and the second slow, with an unexpected return to his old preoccupation with tone-color. The orchestration is transparent; it does not exploit the mass of the orchestral body, but has instead a kind of light polyphony and a beautiful, airy resonance.[6]

Tre Ricercari (1938), written in the tradition of the Brandenburg Concertos, is the culmination of many years of preparatory work. It was commissioned for the Music Festival in Venice, and various circumstances obliged Martinů to write it very quickly. The title is an original term for an instrumental piece written in direct imitation of the motet technique which in the seventeenth century merged with the fugue.

This example from the second movement (Largo) appears

[5] Henri Prunières in *Le Temps*.
[6] It is unfortunate that this score, like so many others of Martinů's compositions, is at present in occupied Europe, inaccessible to free orchestras. All of Martinů's work is prohibited by the Nazis in the occupied countries.

complicated in the score, but is in reality extremely quiet and lyrical:

In this movement there is a passage played by three violins and three cellos which, through slight harmonic nuances, attains a very free atmosphere:

The genesis of this perfect work is quite characteristic of the composer's artistic workshop. He did not begin it with any enthusiasm, and at first was not at all satisfied with what he had written. The style, of a melodic, almost Italian nature, seemed strange even to him; and at its Paris performance the conductor, Charles Munch, though a personal friend of his, admitted that he felt very much the same about it. However, an American musician, Leopold Mannes, who was present at the Venice performance was fascinated by the composition, and never failed to speak of it in glowing terms whenever he met one of Martinů's compatriots. The reaction of the public in Venice and Paris was very similar; from the first measures the attention of the audience was held with growing intensity until the end of the work. At first sight the score looks somewhat complicated, and the part-writing actually is so. In performance, however, the sound is extremely pure, simple, and full of beauty, as is also the structure. *Tre Ricercari* is absolute music — a true modern counterpart to the Brandenburg Concertos. It takes twelve minutes to play, and is scored for three violins, three cellos, flute, two oboes, two bassoons, two trumpets, and two pianos.

8 : Realization: Concerto Grosso — Double Concerto

M ARTINŮ and his wife had found it necessary, for one reason or another, to change their living-quarters several times during the preceding years. Not long after their marriage in 1931 they went to live in a miniature house in the artists' colony on the rue de Vanves and remained there for two or three years. Later they stayed six months in the Montrouge suburb, not far from the Porte de Chatillon. Finally they settled in the avenue du Parc Montsouris, where they had two small attic rooms, very hot in the summer and cold in the winter. It was here, in 1938, that Martinů began work on his Concerto Grosso after completing the *Tre Ricercari*. By this time his tendency towards absolute music had become clearly evident. This is best explained by the following notes that he wrote for the program of the Boston Symphony, which performed the work under Serge Koussevitzky on November 14, 1941:

The title "Concerto Grosso" bespeaks my leaning toward this form, which occupies a position between chamber music and symphonic music. It will be evident that I have not followed the traditional form of "concerto grosso" but rather the characteristic alternations of "soli" and "tutti," which I have given to the pianos, woodwinds, and strings. The violins are divided into three sections in order to diffuse [1] the full sonority of the strings and to provide more polyphonic activity. I am reluctant to make an analysis of the form, which offers no real help toward the understanding of a new work. I prefer that the public listen instead of constantly asking, "When does the second theme come in? Is this the development already, or is it still the exposition?" The form should be felt through the development of the ideas and through the internal structure of the work, which represents a certain attitude of the composer, and that attitude should make itself known clearly without explanations. In the first movement, I work with a little rhythmic germ of a half-measure which binds the different developments of the other motives and which appears in the most diversified forms up to the end, where there remains nothing but this little germ within the fullness of the orchestra. The Andante of the second movement is an extended song by the violoncellos and the other strings, which continues forceful and expressive. But a few measures before the end, the song subsides into tranquility. In the third movement, of lively character, the two pianos take the foremost place as soloists, setting forth the themes (somewhat rhythmic) of a "Rondo." At first they are enveloped always by the polyphony of the orchestra; then the orchestra takes them up, relegating the contrapuntal ornamentation to the pianos.

Misfortune has dogged this work ever since its composition. Plans for having it published in Vienna (Universal Edition) were frustrated by the *Anschluss*, and the Paris première scheduled for the same year had to be canceled since the score and orchestral material could not be obtained in time from Vienna. It was to have been performed in Prague by the Czech Philharmonic under Václav Talich in 1938, but the Munich crisis intervened. Finally Charles Munch in Paris overcame the technical difficulties and set the date of the première for May 1940. This time military events took a hand. Then, while Martinů was fleeing Paris, the manuscript of the Concerto Grosso was lost. On his arrival in America he was surprised

---

[1] In the French original Martinů wrote "to crumble the conventionally 'rich' sonorities of the strings."

with the news that a copy of the score was already here. George Szell had rescued it from Prague and brought it via Australia to New York. Finally Serge Koussevitzky performed the work with the Boston Symphony Orchestra in Boston on November 14, 1941. During the same season it was repeated in New York, and since then has been played several times. Its success is always immediate and overwhelming.

At its New York performance the following year the Concerto Grosso was received, according to the press, "with a prolonged ovation," and "the listeners were immediately enraptured. . . . The neo-classic novelty . . . though modern in content, had an authentic early eighteenth century atmosphere, seldom so closely approximated in contemporary attempts in the genre." [2]

The Double Concerto, the most forceful of all Martinů's works, was started during the summer of 1938 at Vieux Moulin and completed in Switzerland in the autumn of 1938. In this he brought the concerto-grosso form to the highest expression it has yet reached in contemporary music. Without doubt its composition was influenced by political events involving his homeland. In July 1938 Martinů went to Prague for the annual festival of the Sokols, an event that he never missed. Soon after this he left for Paris, filled with courage and joy at the vitality of his countrymen and of the Czechoslovak Republic. In September he and his wife accepted an invitation to visit Switzerland. "We lived," Martinů recalls, [3]

. . . in the mountains, almost completely isolated from the outside world — in a countryside full of sunlight and the song of birds — while somewhere in Europe the great tragedy that was relentlessly approaching the frontiers of my homeland was being prepared. With

---

[2] Noel Straus in the *New York Times* of January 11, 1942. This quotation shows the public response to Martinů's works, and how quickly and easily he makes contact with an audience. See also the *New York Herald Tribune* and *World-Telegram* of January 11 and 12, 1942.

[3] In his article published in the Czech daily of New York, *New Yorské Listy*, on April 12, 1942.

anguish we listened every day to the news bulletins on the radio, trying to find encouragement and hope that did not come. The clouds were quickly gathering and becoming steadily more threatening. During this time I was at work on the Double Concerto; but all my thoughts and longings were constantly with my endangered country, where only a few months before I had been filled with such hope and joy by the unforgettable moments of the Sokol Festival. Now, in the lonely mountainous countryside, echoed the sound of my piano, filled with sorrow and pain but also with hope. Its notes sang out the feelings and sufferings of all those of our people who, far away from their home, were gazing into the distance and seeing the approaching catastrophe. So strongly did this feeling break out in my composition that a year later, at the first performance of the Double Concerto,[4] the critics spoke of the tragedy of Czechoslovakia in connection with my work; and at the end of the performance the entire hall spontaneously demonstrated its sympathies. It is a composition written under terrible circumstances, but the emotions it voices are not those of despair but rather of revolt, courage, and unshakable faith in the future. These are expressed by sharp, dramatic shocks, by a current of tones that never ceases for an instant, and by a melody that passionately claims the right to freedom. There was not a man in the audience who was not touched by this musical language.

The Geneva critic R. Aloys Mooser wrote in *La Suisse*, on the day following the performance, this eloquent appreciation of Martinů's most nearly perfect orchestral work:

We find in the "Double Concerto" miraculous fantasy, irresistible dynamism, and an exceptional sense of constructivism. But we also find here a tragic sentiment and fascinating expression in which this talent attains its ripeness, today in full blossom. For there springs forth the most authentic and generous music in such abundance and with such great force that it leaves us astonished. This is music that follows its own path, that does not owe anybody anything, that does not for a moment hesitate, and that continually renews itself.

This composition, which surprisingly has not as yet been performed in America, is so significant in Martinů's entire

---

[4] In Basel, Switzerland, on February 9, 1940, given by Paul Sacher and his Kammerorchester.

work that it warrants further quotations from Swiss papers. The music critic of the *Basler Nachrichten* (February 12, 1940) calls the Double Concerto "a full gearing with the drama of the present." He continues: "We know of the Czech composer Smetana that he wrote his music as a true patriot; in the case of his modern compatriot we also discern this warm sympathy for the fate of his homeland." The *Basler Volksblatt* of the same date says: "This work demonstrates how the contrapuntal tangle of musical speech is being freed by the vivacity of the Czech temperament; and how a clear and characteristic profile of thematic ideas — with all their harmonic daring — can be justified and made comprehensible. And, finally, how this boldness is entirely in the service of a forceful personal expression, thus completing the artistic cycle."

Further testimony to the effect of the work, this time of a personal nature, was given by Arthur Honegger, whose *Prelude, arioso et fughette sur le nom de Bach* was given at the same concert in Basel. At the conclusion of the performance of Double Concerto Honegger, who was standing in a group of friends, began to beat his breast, exclaiming: "It's suffocating me, I shall explode." He embraced Martinů, and after calming down a little declared: "I must seem to you like an idiot — but I have to cry. That is the way music should affect its listeners."

There was also another little dramatic incident in connection with the performance of the Double Concerto. The forty musicians, members of the Basel Kammerorchester, absolutely refused after the first reading to rehearse the work any further because it seemed to them too complicated. Paul Sacher, the conductor, in an attempt to make them change their minds, said: "Gentlemen, you do not realize that you have in front of you a chef-d'œuvre." Finally they reluctantly agreed to continue, and there were six months of arduous rehearsals. At the

47

performance, in the New Basel Theater, the first movement had hardly begun before the entire audience underwent a change and remained completely rapt and fascinated until the last note, when their enthusiasm broke out as though it were the release of tension after a storm.

It is difficult to say just where the strength of the Double Concerto lies. Honegger on one occasion began to debate this question, asking: "Is it the melody? Is it the rhythm? Is it the technique — the dissonance — the tonality — the atonality? . . . No," he ended by saying, "it is everything together. This new music has a direct and amazing appeal."

In view of the truth of Honegger's remark, an excerpt from the Double Concerto obviously can show merely one isolated aspect of this complex work. The following is from the first movement:

The main theme, which appears here in two-part polyphony, is later repeated with full orchestra in the coda of the third movement:

Here is an interesting excerpt from the second movement:

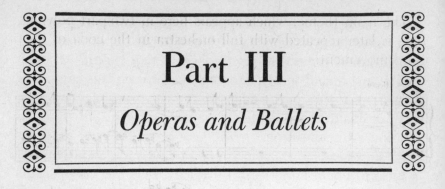

Part III
Operas and Ballets

9 : Early Stage Works

MARTINŮ'S compositions for the theater do not represent any one period in his work. His first important ballet, *Istar*, was written in Prague in 1921, and his great opera *Juliette* in Paris in 1937. In the years between these two works he composed seven operas, nine ballets, and three short operas for radio, as well as music for motion pictures.

Since his early youth Martinů had been gradually preparing himself for his work in connection with the stage. We remember how as a child he first came into contact with the theater, and how much time he devoted to attending plays and the opera during his student years in Prague; also the orchestral composition he wrote in those days to Maeterlinck's play for marionettes, and his plans for composing an opera with words by Przybyszewski. His two early attempts at ballet, both of which are now lost, have also been mentioned, and the music he improvised for students' productions in Polička. To Martinů the main interest of the theater lies in the stage performance rather than in the psychology of the drama. Though he had written songs since boyhood — not to mention his successful cantata, *Czech Rhapsody* — he was not satisfied with these. Ballet gave him for the time being the opportunity for

50

scenic work and the solution of the stage problems which so fascinated him. In fact, it gave him a better opportunity than would have been possible with opera at that time.

His first opera, *The Soldier and the Dancer*, was composed in Paris between 1926 and 1927, on a theme suggested by a play of Plautus. The original libretto was written by J. L. Budín,[1] a Czech satirical writer, and revised several times on lines suggested by Martinů. The work, which is an attempt at a modern opera buffa, is in three acts. It is not entirely uniform in style, and owes something to Stravinsky's *History of a Soldier*.

Collaboration with the French poet Ribemont-Dessaignes, which followed immediately after this, produced three operas — one quite short, the others full-length works. These are more interesting when looked upon as preparing the way for Martinů's future scenic works than in themselves. The first, *The Tears of the Knife*, was commissioned for the Festival of Modern Music in Baden-Baden in 1928; but Martinů's friends there were so much taken aback by the fantastic libretto — in which a corpse is suspended on the stage for the entire act — that they had not the courage to produce it. In its place they played Martinů's *Entr'acte* (Three Pieces for chamber orchestra), and the opera has never been performed. The failure of Ribemont-Dessaignes's libretto in no way worried Martinů; he continued with their collaboration, having a great admiration for the language and style of his French friend, as well as for his eccentric imagination. Themes of this kind were much more to the liking of the composer than those of the more conventional drama, and he was constantly looking for plays that would give the audience a feeling of the stage rather than of real life.

Martinů had been originally attracted to the writings of Ribemont-Dessaignes — who is the author of the unusual

[1] This was the pseudonym of Mr. Jan Löwenbach.

novel *Frontières humaines* — because of his startling gift for capturing individual phases of thought and making them suddenly present the normal mind in an entirely new light. These changes are, to a certain extent, the subject of Martinů's second opera, *Life's Hardships*. Based on the fairy-tale *Three Wishes*, it is an attempt at an opera film, and makes full use of all the modern devices of the stage. We find here song, spoken prose, recitative, and pantomime. Two situations are presented simultaneously, the real and the fantastic — the actual existence of the character taking place on the stage, while his imaginary life is projected on a screen in the background. With Ribemont-Dessaignes he also worked on *The Day of Kindness*, which is based on a theme by the well-known Russian novelist Ilya Ehrenburg. This is a satire on the so-called kindness of philanthropic ladies during the first World War, and is on the same lines as *Life's Hardships*. Here two country boys take the aforesaid kindness seriously, and their illusions are confronted with concrete experience. From the musical point of view also, *Day of Kindness*, of which Martinů wrote only two acts, is in the same category as *Life's Hardships*. As was said before, these three operas, while representing Martinů's fruitful collaboration with French writers and his interest in international literature, are to be looked upon chiefly as preparing the way for more important work.

During the period after *Istar* he composed six ballets, in which his development in variety of ideas and skill in scenic realization can be plainly followed. One of these, written in 1923, is called *Who Is the Most Powerful in the World?* It is the story of some mice who are trying to answer the question in the title. Is it the sun? No, the clouds can hide it, and the wind can disperse the clouds, but the wind is helpless against a strong wall. Mice, however, can undermine a wall — therefore, mice are the most powerful in the world! Martinů was working in secret on this ballet at the time when he was unsuccessfully studying with Josef Suk at the Prague Conservatory. The première was given at the National Theater in Brno (Brünn) in 1924 on the same program as Leoš Janáček's opera about animals, *Cunning Little Fox*, both works being conducted by František Neumann. The pianist Rudolf Firkušný, who sat in Janáček's box on this occasion, relates how the older composer followed the performance of Martinů's ballet very attentively, and at the end was heard to remark: "Why should the rooster in Martinů's ballet have a better costume than any in *Cunning Little Fox*?"

The ballet *Revolt* is a satire on jazz and modern music in general. In this there is a revolution of the notes, and in the end a young girl brings peace by singing a simple folk-song. Another, *Le Raid merveilleux*, is a mechanical ballet without any living characters. An airplane takes the central part, and a propeller and scenes of countryside and ocean are also included.

10 : Špaliček

IN his desire to return to the true sources of the theater and overcome influences such as the Ibsen drama Martinů, though away from his homeland, now reverted to Czech folklore, legends, and fairy-tales. *Špaliček* [1] — or "Czech ballet," as he calls it in a subtitle — is drawn from this inexhaustible treasure-house, and is his first big scenic work. He wrote it in 1931, and it clearly shows his growing independence.

---

[1] Literally *Špaliček* means "little club." In Bohemia, many decades ago, it was a collection of folk-songs, published at first on four-page sheets and sold at fairs. Later these songs were incorporated into books called *Špaliček*.

The fact that after ten years of search and of collaboration with ultra-modern, almost dadaesque librettists Martinů resorted to folklore is very characteristic of him. In view of his special love for old music it might appear more likely that he would have been influenced by the madrigal dramas of the sixteenth century, or even the *sacre rappresentazioni* of the middle of the fifteenth century — in short, that he would follow the historical development of opera. But to Martinů the history of the theater was more important than the history of opera. Later on he did return — though in a manner all his own — to the "old delineation of episodes in religious history"[2] — in other words, to the Bible and the old French mysteries and miracles. At this time, however, he seemingly deserted universalism in order to come closer to the feelings of the common Czech people; and the musical expression he then discovered differed completely from his preceding style in that it made little use of acquired technique, but was of an extremely simple and modest nature — having no relation at all to the complications of the modern idiom. He had always before him a clearly outlined plan, which was to create a new public and prepare it gradually for a modern Czech opera. His intentions were that the Czech people should become acquainted with the history of the theater as a whole. And in spite of the distance between Paris and Prague he was able, through untiring correspondence and the precise directions in his scores, to succeed in his endeavors.

In *Špaliček* he began to solve many problems and to fill the gaps which various political and cultural circumstances had left in Czech opera and theater. This work is a three-act ballet, with a women's chorus which sings in the orchestra pit. The first act opens with a prologue in which a fairy tells folkstories to a group of children.

---

[2] Paul Bekker: *The Changing Opera* (New York, W. W. Norton).

Scene 1. Rooster and Hen. The Rooster chokes while trying to swallow too large a grain of corn, and needs a drink of water. The Hen begs for some from the spring, the dressmaker, the tailor, etc. Finally water is sent from heaven and the Rooster's life is saved.

Scene 2. The Tale of Puss in Boots.

Scene 3. Children's Games: (a) The game of the maidens.
           (b) The water-sprite.
           (c) The wolf.

Scene 4. The Story of the Magic Sack: A farmer gives some grain to the devil in exchange for a magic sack. He comes to an enchanted castle, where Death (represented by a woman) awaits him; he catches her in his sack, however. From that moment no one dies in the whole world, for Death cannot escape from the sack without the farmer's permission. Many years pass, and one day the farmer — now an old man — is walking towards the gates of hell. But he still does not want to let Death out of his sack; so hell refuses to let him in and he sets out on the road to heaven, where, tired of life, he at last sets her free. He then enters paradise, and Death descends to earth again.

The second act is the classical story of Cinderella, transplanted to a Czech village and varied with folk dances and games.

Scene 1. Death is shown transformed into a straw scarecrow and is carried out of the village by young girls, in celebration of the arrival of spring. Among these girls are Cinderella and her sisters. Their father is returning from town with gifts for his daughters.

Scene 2. The girls are seen dancing and playing the game Queen (folk dance). A fairy arrives and transforms Cinderella into a beautiful lady. Then comes the party given at the castle by the handsome Prince. In the morning he searches the village for Cinderella. Some boys are dancing and playing the game Golden Gate. The Prince tries the slipper on the girls' feet, and finally finds Cinderella.

Scene 3. Village wedding scenes.

Third Act:

Scene 1. The Legend of St. Dorothy. This is a folk-song which for years has been sung in Czech villages. In the story — which is very old, of ancient Roman origin — a young Christian girl prefers death to giving up her religion, and is beheaded. This is played and sung very primitively.

Scene 2. The Legend of the Phantom Bridegroom. A young girl begs the Blessed Virgin to return her dead bridegroom to her. His spirit comes back and drags her off to the cemetery, where the horrified girl saves herself at the last moment by a prayer to the Holy Ghost.[3]

Špaliček is in the form of a revue in which the scenes follow each other in quick succession, and the choreography and music are most effectively combined. It is scored for chamber orchestra, except in the last scene (The Legend of the Phantom Bridegroom), where full orchestra is used. In 1940 Martinů rescored the whole work for large orchestra and changed the original plan for the ballet, enlarging the tale of Puss in Boots and substituting for the Phantom Bridegroom the wedding dances in Act II, Scene 3.

Martinů also composed two one-act operas and a cantata for radio on folk lines, and purposely wrote them in such a way that even small amateur groups could perform them. The operas are *The Voice of the Forest*, with a libretto by the Czech poet Vítězslav Nezval, and *Comedy on the Bridge*, based on an old Czech play of popular character by Klicpera. Both works were performed by Radio Prague and had a great success with the public. In contrast to these the two-part cantata *Kytice* (*Bouquet*) is of more ambitious requirements, being scored for large chorus and ensemble, with two pianos.

---

[3] This tale is also known under the title of *Leonora*, and was adapted in a popular style by the Czech poet K. J. Erben.

11 : Miracle of Our Lady

THE OLD French mystery plays given in front of
Notre Dame inspired in Martinů the wish to write further
scenic works. In 1933 he composed an opera, *The Miracle of
Our Lady*, on a libretto that was of his own arranging except
for the middle part "Mariken de Nimèque"; this, though suggested by him, was arranged by the French poet Henri Ghéon.
The Miracle of Our Lady is in four parts:

First Act:
   1. Prologue — The Wise and Foolish Virgins.
   2. Mariken de Nimèque.
Second Act:
   3. Nativity.
   4. Sister Pascaline.

As is shown in the title, the opera [1] is based on medieval
miracles and mysteries. The Prologue is on words from the
Bible,[2] and "Mariken" is the story of a Flemish miracle. For
the "Nativity" Martinů used a Czech text from folklore collected by František Sušil;[3] and "Sister Pascaline" is a Spanish
legend adapted from the text of Julius Zeyer, the Czech poet.
From the period of *Špaliček* onwards the sequence of events

[1] The Czech title is *Hry o Marii* (*Miracles de Notre Dame* or *Jeux de la Sainte
Vièrge*). It was first performed under this title at the National Theater in Prague
in 1935 (J. Charvát, conductor).
[2] The old French drama of the Wise and Foolish Virgins, with its Latin
choruses and Provençal refrain, is preserved in the Bibliothèque Nationale of Paris.
Martinů naturally saw this document, though his musical conception has nothing
in common with it. In 1938, three years after the première of *The Miracle of Our
Lady*, an adaptation of the madrigal mystery *The Wise and Foolish Virgins*, har-
monized and orchestrated by F. Liuzzi, was performed at the Florence Festival.
Martinů, though present at the Venice Festival of that year, for the performance
of his *Tre Ricercari*, was not in Florence at the time.
[3] F. Sušil was a Czech priest, who collected several volumes of folklore from
Moravia.

in Martinů's libretti is not to be considered actual in a realistic sense; the text is, rather, arranged in such a manner as to create some special effect desired in a given situation. This is also the case in Martinů's employment of folk poetry. These texts have in reality no factual relationship with one another, though they evoke mental pictures emotionally related to the story. For instance, in the scene of "Sister Pascaline" (*The Miracle of Our Lady*) Martinů makes use of a religious text, *Dies Iræ*. Actually, the only everyday words in the entire opera are those spoken by Pascaline when, in answer to voices that call to her from off stage, she replies: "Who is calling?" In the intensely dramatic moment when she is on the scaffold, a great role on the stage is assigned to the chorus, and Pascaline's aria is stripped of all gesticulation, action or emotion, thus all the more eloquently expressing a deep inner feeling. The words of the old Czech folk-song Martinů uses in this scene are practically untranslatable, but possibly some of their strangely poetical quality may be conveyed by the following literal translation:

> O my almighty God,
> Who hath deigned to create me into the world
> like the wild flowers
> that refresh the eyes of the beholder.
> While the years are young
> the flowers bloom for me,
> but when old age comes
> the soul grows afraid.
> It sees grim Death,
> it sees the dreadful missile
> he aims at me,
> the fiery arrow he shoots at me.
> And as the soul leaves the body,
> sadness comes into the heart.
> The Lord will show it
> His pierced hands and feet,

His sacred wounds:
Look, despairing man,
how you neglected your soul,
how much I gave
to deliver you from hell.
But you were not grateful to me
and now must enter eternal fire.
O dear Lord Jesus Christ,
Lead us along the sacred path.

It is quite evident that it would be impossible to act out this text, since it contains no action of any kind. And yet how beautiful it is! The words obviously are the meditations of an old man, thus — according to the standards of conventional opera — being unsuitable for Pascaline, who is a young girl. But the poem is so well known and popular (in other countries also, as is so often the case with folk words) that it makes an infinitely more powerful effect than would be possible with a more stereotyped climax. Not only is the attention of the audience aroused and its emotion heightened by the beauty of the text, in which each word speaks for itself, but the composer is thus able to take advantage of the singer's musical rather than histrionic abilities. In this way it becomes clear that the scene on the scaffold is not one of desperation or even of resignation, but of spiritual purity — something quite new in the field of opera. Actually, Martinů does not regard as perfect the results he has attained with this peculiar and very personal inspiration, and much may yet be expected from him in this particular form of art.[4]

The scenic problems of this important opera are very vital in Martinů's opinion, one of his chief principles being the accenting of theatrical values. While always considering the music of primary importance, he worked simultaneously with

---

[4] I once asked Martinů how he liked the book *Wisdom of China and India*, by Lin Yutang. The laconic reply was: "Very much; each page contains the plot for an opera." On being asked to give an example he replied: "The story of the blind man to whom his fellow men describe a sunrise."

the text, staging, gesture, dance, and all other elements of the performance. Often he broke up a part which would ordinarily have been assigned to one actor, and gave some of it to the chorus and some to the orchestra. The chorus, though appearing on the scene, does not have the role of the usual opera chorus; it takes the place, rather, of the narrator of the story. Martinů compressed sections that would have led to long musical dialogues, and revealed their contents in rapid speech or quick action. He does not follow all the nuances of passion and struggle, but only those that he believes can be expressed in music. In the end the result is poetry. His basic thesis is that the laws and logic of opera are quite different from those of spoken drama; he feels that when too much stress is put on the literal meaning of words, their poetry is lost and the opera suffers in its freedom of action. In this Martinů resembles Soni of Florence, who in the year 1640 wrote of the origin of the operatic form:

"The one thing everyone agreed on was that, since the music of the day was quite inadequate to the expression of the words, and its development actually repugnant to the thought, means must be found in the attempt to bring music back to that of classical times, to bring out the chief melody prominently so that the poetry should be clearly intelligible." [5]

In *The Miracle of Our Lady* Martinů tries to express in his music as much as possible of the essential poetic content of the text, while always maintaining a primary interest in the unity of the musical conception, which he never sacrifices to considerations of action or characterization. To him an opera does not present a philosophical or psychological problem. It is a spectacle transformed by music. He departs from the realistic conception of the plot and does everything to point out that the opera is not a fragment of real life, but a theatrical

[5] Quoted from *The International Cyclopedia of Music and Musicians*, article "Opera," by Oscar Thompson (New York: Dodd, Mead & Company; 1939).

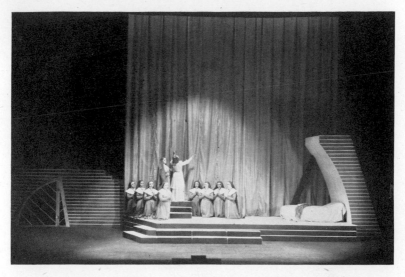

SCENE FROM *THE MIRACLE OF OUR LADY*

SCENE FROM *SUBURBAN THEATRE*

performance. His "Notes to the opera *The Miracle of Our Lady*," written for the first performance in Prague on March 9, 1934, constitute an important key to his operatic work as well as to his whole philosophy of music. Excerpts from the notes follow:

If we follow the problems and psychological processes of the theatre we find that opera today identifies itself to a considerable extent with the spoken drama. For this reason it is impossible to give it a form of its own, for in stressing the spoken word opera loses its strength, its freedom of action, and even its *raison d'être*.

The functions of speech and singing differ greatly; and though by employing the methods of spoken drama we may approach it in verisimilitude, we leave the true realm of opera. Too great a dependence upon the meaning of the spoken word — which in singing often becomes incomprehensible — deprives the opera of clarity. To save the situation recitative is often resorted to, which is a very poor substitute for direct speech, and only ends by becoming boring.

The elasticity of the spoken word, containing as it does its own melodic and rhythmic shadings, is in itself so varied that music can hardly improve upon it; in stressing it musical lyricism is lost. We then try to fill the gaps with a certain surface agitation which is mere meaningless noise and far away from true music.

Similarly, action is not the same in spoken drama as in opera, where it is sometimes delayed by the singing and replaced by a musical extension — a lyric or dramatic passage inserted into the work during which action partly or altogether ceases. And though by obeying the laws of spoken drama we may occasionally preserve a purely musical expression it is not always in the interests of the work.

The moment music is employed to interpret emotions which it is not equipped to do, it loses its character and sincerity and becomes a mere accompaniment. A singer is able to express dramatic intensity only up to a certain point, beyond which it must be reinforced by the orchestra. The singer then strains his voice, loses his concept of the music, and his singing changes into unmusical noise. In this way the dramatic element may be heightened, but the musical element is often completely lost. The action leaves the stage and descends into the orchestra pit, the audience then having the impression that instead of assisting at a dramatic representation it is at a concert.

When I began to write *The Miracle of Our Lady* one of my primary intentions was to make the most of the theatrical elements — to depart from logic and stress improbabilities. Furthermore, another conviction that I followed was a determination not to transcend the limits of a noble and serene musical expression. No dramatic or passionate moment must be allowed to break out of bounds of the beauty in music. Such an arrangement may lack a dramatically heightened climax, but it gains in balance and order. Naturally, I arranged the scenes in such a manner as to enable me to make the most of their musical possibilities. But conception changes everything; and as my play does not deal with reality and does not follow the customary logical procedure, it attains freedom according to my musical and scenic ideas.

12 : Juliette

THE SUCCESS of *The Miracle of Our Lady* in Prague was great. But Martinů did not rest on his laurels, and within three years had already produced another opera — this time of a completely different type. It is *Suburban Theater*, a Czech *commedia dell' arte*, in which he uses not only folk texts but selections from Molière and sketches by the famous French mime Jean-Gaspard Deburau — who, by the way, was born in Bohemia. The first act is a ballet and the second and third are opera; and the plot of the ballet in the first act is repeated in the opera of the second and third acts, ending with a Rossini-like vocal ensemble. *Suburban Theater* — a sort of entertaining interlude between *The Miracle of Our Lady* and Martinů's next full-length opera, *Juliette* — was inspired by the French Théâtre de la Foire and the popular plays of the Paris Boulevard du Crime, to which he had been drawn by his technical interest in the theater. These plays, in which

Deburau often took part, were given at the beginning of the nineteenth century in the Théâtre des Funambules, where they were attended by Alfred de Musset, Georges Sand, and many other writers of those times. From Molière Martinů took a scene out of *The Flying Doctor* (*Le Médecin volant*), in which a boy plays a double role: jumping in at the window, he impersonates a doctor; jumping out again, he returns to his own character. Apart from this the opera is really a series of folk episodes interspersed with some tricks and gags borrowed from Deburau. The main roles are Pierrot, Harlequin, Columbine, the Burgomaster of a town, and an innkeeper, with barmaids. The whole piece, which is of a humorous nature throughout, is light and sparkling, with recitativo secco reminiscent of the classical composers of Mozart's time; and the accompaniment and intermezzi, for chamber orchestra in which strings predominate, are simply and delicately scored.

Martinů's operatic masterpiece, *Juliette, or the Key to Dreams*, written in 1936 and 1937, is a full-length opera with a unified libretto adapted from a play of the same name by the French writer Georges Neveux.[1] In *Juliette* Martinů departs

---

[1] It happened in 1932 that I invited Martinů to a performance of the play *Juliette* at the Théâtre de l'Avenue in Paris (with Mlle Falconetti in the part of Juliette), and on this occasion introduced him to my friend Neveux. Georges Neveux originally studied law, his father wishing him to become a judge. For a short while he practiced this profession, but at the time of his meeting with Martinů he was already known as a lyric poet, and was also active as secretary of the Comédie des Champs-Élysées (Louis Jouvet, director). Collaboration between Neveux and Martinů proved to be ideal. Martinů found in *Juliette* a perfect libretto and adapted it for opera. By mutual agreement the play remained as it was except for the ending, in which Michel is unable to decide whether to enter for ever the "Office of Dreams," and the curtain falls. In the opera Michel is also undecided, but makes up his mind on hearing the theme of Juliette. Neveux was present at the première of the opera in Prague. Years later Martinů asked him what his impression had been, and Neveux replied, in a manner all his own: "Terrible!" By this he meant that on hearing the opera he had realized for the first time the inadequacy of his own words when divorced from the music that so perfectly expressed all the nuances of unreality in the story. This was particularly evident in the third act, which was unsuccessful in the play, though exceptionally impressive in the opera.

from the folk type of composition. The theme is the confronting of reality with the illusion of a dream.

In the story Michel, a bookseller who lives in a small town near the sea, hears one evening the sound of a young girl's singing coming from an open window on the market-place. Later, when he is in Paris, he returns to this memory in a dream, during the course of which he searches for the girl and finally finds her. But, as happens in dreams, the little town by the sea seems to have changed completely. Its inhabitants have no memory, their entire life being a chain of new events and unforeseen situations having no relation with the past. In his dream Michel wanders around the town, the only person who knows what he wants and why he came there. The whole story, accordingly, is one of fantasy; and it was this quality in Neveux's play that most attracted Martinů. Laws of real life and logic are here set aside, and in their place appears a dream logic — much more exact, and intensely poetic. When Michel, who in dreams is in love with Juliette, enters into reality, he finds that real life is a disappointment; so he too loses his memory. In the "Office of Dreams" of the third act anyone may purchase a ticket to a dream, simply leaving when the dream is over. Some people remain there permanently and become insane. Michel, although he sees these insane people, cannot make up his mind whether to stay or leave until in the end he hears from far away the theme of Juliette, which draws him back to the city of dreams. The opera ends without a finale or climax of any kind. Here reality is the reality of dreamland, of irrational spiritual emotions; but, contrary to the psychological drama that Martinů so much dislikes, theatrical effects are not expressed in a conventional manner but by new and varied arrangements on the stage. In plot the opera is somewhat similar to Julian Green's novel *Midnight*, in which the fantastic diary of the dreams of two lovers is so convincing that the reader cannot but believe it.

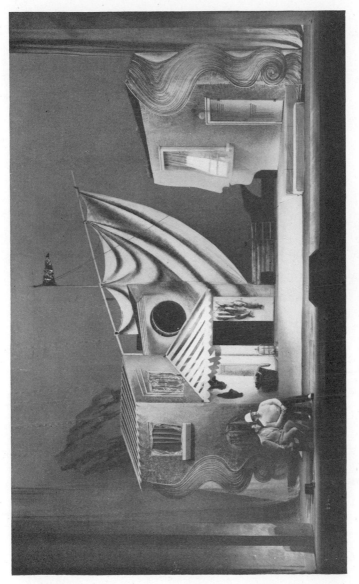

SCENE FROM JULIETTE

When Martinů read the book of *Juliette* he was even more impressed by the beauty of Neveux's language than when he heard it on the stage. He began to compose his opera to the French text, which he rearranged to suit his melodic line and his feeling of musical logic. As the work was to be produced in Prague, however, it would have to be sung in Czech. He therefore made an attempt at translation, only to find that the music would not now fit the Czech words, thus necessitating the complete rewriting of all that he had already composed. The reverse would occur in any translation of the libretto back into the original French.

In this work Martinů returns, for almost the first time since *La Bagarre*, to the use of a large orchestra. The singing parts are in a style that may be termed "spoken melos." Though the whole opera contains only one really songful passage, sung by Juliette, its impression on the listeners is of true singing. The vocal writing is nowhere subservient to recitation and yet every word can be understood. The music is ever flowing, the individual parts returning only in accordance with certain scenic situations and in no way disturbing the continuity of the work; on the contrary, they support it. *Juliette* is a lyric poem, without dramatic effects. The singers therefore cannot indulge in the conventional operatic gestures. False theatricalism disappears and what remains is absolute freedom of action. There is no singing chorus in *Juliette*, its place being taken by ensembles of solo singers who are heard from behind the scenes, from the windows of village houses, and so on. The work has no great love scene in the conventional operatic sense; nevertheless the whole second act is in itself one long love scene, in a new and more natural sense — set in an echoing, scented forest, and surrounded by an atmosphere of enchantingly beautiful music. Practically all the operatic conventions are abandoned; yet the center of gravity is always on the stage and not in the orchestra. There are even a few spoken passages in *Juliette*, both with and without music, though the main substance is in "melos." Unity of the arts, as Wagner understood it, simply does not exist here: action, ballet, and orchestra are separated. But in the whole realm of modern opera there are few works of greater artistic intensity and essential unity. *Juliette* is the best possible illustration of the fact that Martinů's operatic principles are exactly opposite to those of Wagner. He avoids extremes of pathos, relying instead on a logical development of the themes, musically controlled. He does not use leitmotives or rapidly changing musical atmosphere to reflect shifting moods in the drama, but follows a constructive plan for the whole opera.

The use of piano alone in the forest scene in order to express something far away — a memory, an echo — shows Martinů's very personal operatic method. It creates exactly the right atmosphere of unreality during a recitative in which a wineseller in a corner of the forest is telling a fantastic story to an old man and his wife who are passing by.

Below are three examples taken from the piano solo played during this recitative: [2]

[2] Since the score of *Juliette* is in occupied Europe, these examples are given from the recollection of Rudolf Firkušný, the Czech pianist now in America. He has on many occasions played the entire piano interlude (without the recitatives) at his recitals under the title of *Juliette*.

66

This theme reappears in the full orchestra in the second act when Michel is losing his memory and entering into dreams.

The interpretation of *Juliette* proved a great success, largely due to the skill and sympathy of the conductor, Václav Talich, supported by Martinů's group of Prague collaborators. Every year the composer had returned to Prague, and there gradually organized an *équipe* (stage director, scene director, choreographer, etc.) who in his absence would be able to present his works according to his intentions. A glance at the careful instructions in the scores of Martinů's operas shows how thoroughly he understands the theater, and how highly developed is his feeling for drama. Jindřich Honzl, one of the finest Czech stage directors, conjured into existence on the stage every detail of Martinů's wishes. In short, it was a perfect performance, and the impression left in Prague by *Juliette* was that it inaugurated a new epoch in modern Czech opera.[3]

One main principle is clearly evident in the entire operatic

---

[3] *Juliette* was rehearsed at the National Theater in Prague for a period of six months. The reason it was possible to devote so much time to the preparation of a new work is that the National Theater is a State institution. In order to maintain its high standard, the State assigns it an annual subsidy of 18 million Czechoslovak crowns (almost 600,000 dollars at the current rate of exchange, though over one million dollars according to the standards of those days).

work of Martinů: he does not try to describe in words the psychology of individual characters on the stage, nor does he arrange his text with regard to the time element; on the contrary, he disregards it in his stressing of the action. The audience is made to join in — as in the popular French theater, where actors are sometimes warned of approaching danger by the reactions in the auditorium. In conventional opera a recitative often tells what is about to happen. Martinů prefers to get the same effect without too much conversation, and therefore selects words which in themselves represent action or the stressing of action rather than explanation. He does his utmost to change the worn-out standards of opera technique which have been so skillfully caricatured by René Clair in his film *Le Million*. And by taking the situation into his own hands he has helped to gain freedom not only for the stage but for music.

Part IV

World Revolution

13 : War

MARTINŮ'S interest in political and social problems was always very great, though he took no personal part in either. He looked at public life from the point of view of the artist, who by creating does his share in contributing towards the general welfare. All the same, he felt more strongly than most people that, just as in music, so in the whole social and political life of the world something was out of order. He fully agreed with the French writer [1] who said at that time: "The hour of fantasy has gone and the problems of life present themselves; and if art does not wish to be brushed aside together with other futilities it must surrender its peripheric adventures and lay firmer foundations. In other words, if art does not find a simpler and more human way to express itself — if it limits itself to satisfying the desires of a questionable luxury — its rights and its prestige risk the loss of their dignity." The more Martinů's fears grew, the more urgently he tried to fulfill what he felt to be his mission in art. And instead of being discouraged he was driven by his creative power and keen insight towards new constructive work.

---

[1] Jean Schlumberger in an article published in *La Nouvelle Revue Française*, quoted from the book *Jalons* (New York: Brentano's; 1941).

However, his interests did not lie in music only; he also earnestly studied the writings of the time in which the collapse of Western civilization was foreshadowed. Oswald Spengler and other writers of philosophic-historic literature found in Martinů an attentive, critical, and thoughtful reader. He is not interested in mere historical data or in the superficial structure of man-made institutions; but he has a thorough knowledge of the main currents of European affairs from the artistic and spiritual point of view. He feels that the ideal of every artist should be to give — in his own way — his very best towards the common cause. What he was constantly looking for was a common denominator — a firm ideology on which modern society could agree and in which art could find a fertile soil.

The fact that the post-war world lacked this common basis and was ruled by selfishness, lack of discipline, and shortsightedness became every day clearer to Martinů. With the Czech philosopher Emanuel Rádl, he saw clearly that the whole structure of modern society was very unstable and that a great deal of constructive thought and labor would be needed to replace outworn conventions by a spiritual authority that should be more human, effective, and lasting. He did not, however, feel the mission of the artist to lie in a utilitarian opportunism or a service of compromise with the times and their immediate necessities. He stood for disinterested collaboration rather than for any conscious effort towards the creation of social art. But he wanted to have the artist's task clearly defined, as in the Gothic period — only from the human point of view rather than the religious.

In this inner struggle Martinů is a true son of the Czech nation, to which the greatest modern Czech — Thomas G. Masaryk — has given a historic mission in a most constructive and human program. When questioned on the meaning of the history of the Czechoslovak nation, Masaryk replied that it lies in its participation in the world's struggle for truth, righteousness, and humanity; and that this participation is neither an act of romanticism nor the result of religious teaching, but a logical outcome of its own national and human capacities. Masaryk, in the words of Romain Rolland, was a master builder who with a firm hand constructed the vault of a cathedral which was hanging over a precipice — able to accomplish this task because of his perfect sense of the balance of pressure and counter-pressure.

These principles of Masaryk may be applied to Martinů's work, with only this difference: that Martinů lived to see the catastrophe. But what Martinů feared was not war; he was a born fighter, if the fight was just and well fought. What he feared was the collapse and loss of all that he held most precious in life. He lived to see this tragedy in the fall of France. Few can have had such a reaction to this terrible, unbelievable event as was his. During his escape from Paris to southern France all that had gone before and all that he had striven for during his whole life vanished from his mind. In Bermuda, where he arrived on March 29, 1941, after ten months of great hardships, it seemed to him as though the countryside, the people, and life in general were all unreal. For there he had once again the feeling of being in a free country, among free people — a feeling that, under the strain of all his difficulties in France, had almost vanished from his life.[2]

The spiritual Calvary that the war brought to Martinů began in the autumn of 1938, during the time of Munich. As we have seen, he reacted towards this period by writing, while on a visit to Switzerland, his most powerful orchestral work, the Double Concerto. His return to Paris was very sad. But his artistic reactions to the tragedy of his own country were posi-

---

[2] He tells about it in the article already quoted from the Czech daily *New Yorské Listy*, April 12, 1941.

tive. Again he reverted to the musical culture of the Czech people — to folklore. In Sušil's collection he found texts for two books of *Madrigals for Six Voices*, which he composed while staying with his wife's family in Vieux Moulin, not far north of Paris. This is a small village, almost lost in the immense forests of Compiègne. Here Martinů was able to work in peace and gather strength on his long, lonely walks through the woods. Walking has always been one of his favorite pursuits, because in this way he is able to pursue his meditations undisturbed. The *Madrigals* are six short pieces for women's voices, some for two, others for more, up to six voices. They are characteristically Czech in feeling, though freely contrapuntal in true madrigal style.

The winter months of the year 1940 were one of the worst periods in Martinů's life. "My spiritual disposition is such," he wrote in one of his letters to America,[3] "that I would rather let everything go. . . . I keep thinking of Prague and our countrymen and of how they must be feeling. It would be better if we did not have to think at all. I have no coal and I cannot work. Here in France everything is slowly disintegrating so that one cannot help being sad. Still, there is the will to work and also the possibility here." Martinů's many friends in Prague tried to get him to return and accept a position as professor at the Prague Conservatory. Instead of this he began to study English, all his thoughts now being centered on his intention of leaving for America, where President Beneš had already arrived and where Martinů, too, wanted to help in the task of awakening the world on behalf of his martyred homeland. "For the time being I have put composition aside," he wrote later. "Somehow I am a different man." He was given courage by the thought that "they are thinking of us at home, counting on us . . . and we cannot and must

---

[3] As is evident from the quotations, these are excerpts from letters written to me.

not disappoint them." For America he was preparing a series of plans. He wished to dedicate to the American people a Czech composition — new "Slavonic Dances," or a symphony. In the meanwhile all performances of his works in Prague were forbidden by the Nazis, who also blocked the fees from his international royalties.

The success of the Double Concerto when it was given in Basel in February 1940, and the response of the public to this "full gearing with the drama of the present," brought encouragement to Martinů; but he found himself unable to concentrate on any new composition. However, he occupied himself with technical work. He revised his ballet *Špalíček* and rewrote it for large orchestra, also doing the same with his Cello Concerto; and he arranged three fragments from *Juliette* for concert performance. Finally he gathered enough energy to write something new, and produced his *Field Mass (La Messe aux Champs d'Honneur)*, dedicated to the Czechoslovak Army volunteers. At the time that he wrote this work he was still obsessed by the thought of the occupation of his homeland; and this is a military rather than a liturgical Mass, and must be given in the open. "The *Field Mass*," writes Martinů,[4] "was written to be performed out of doors — under the sky and clouds that unite us with the soldiers at the front as well as with our compatriots at home." He was at that time one of a group, which included many Czech artists living in Paris, who were pooling their individual talents in order to organize entertainment for the Czechoslovak soldiers. They planned to write short plays such as the soldiers themselves could perform, and in addition prepared broadcasts and arranged folk choruses for them to sing. The text of the *Field Mass* is from folk poetry and was arranged by Martinů himself, with the collaboration of Jiří Mucha. It contains many lyrical passages

---

[4] Quoted from the article in the *New Yorské Listy*, April 12, 1941.

which speak of the memories of a soldier on guard and his longing for home, and there are moments of defiance, with stirring expressions of steadfastness and a firm faith in victory. The work, which is full of trumpet calls and the beating of drums, ends with quotations from the Psalms. It is scored for men's chorus, baritone solo, two piccolos, two clarinets, three trumpets, two trombones, piano, harmonium, and percussion.

Although at about this time Martinů also wrote a *Military March* for the Czechoslovak Army Band in France, he did not allow political and military developments to divert the main stream of his creative work. In the winter of 1940 he composed one of his best chamber works, the First Sonata for cello and piano, the manuscript of which is unfortunately at this moment inaccessible somewhere in France. This is in sharp contrast to compositions of the type of *Tre Ricercari*, for it is full of spontaneous intensity, passionate and singing. The first movement is particularly dramatic, though it interprets the sonata form not so much in the romantic as in the original sense, as it was before the time of Beethoven. The second movement (Adagio) includes a masterly cadenza for the cello; and the third movement is a rhythmic and dynamic Rondo. The cello part, written throughout with exceptional skill, employs to the full all the technical resources of the instrument. Pierre Fournier and Rudolf Firkušný played this sonata at the last concert of the Société pour la Musique Contemporaine (formerly Triton) in Paris on May 19, 1940, in the hall of Archives de Danses. The atmosphere at the performance was unusually moving, for at that time everyone was breathless with tension over the uncertainty of France's fate; and the heartfelt demonstrations of the audience were as much a tribute to a Czech artist as to his great and forceful composition. Those were wonderful moments in the life of Martinů, in spite of the war. He and his wife lived at that time in the rue des Marroniers, and many a congenial group of friends and musicians would meet in their apartment after these concerts, which for fear of air raids were held in the morning. But this period lasted only a short time; three weeks after the performance of the Cello Sonata Martinů had already fled from Paris.

14 : Homeless

MARTINŮ and his wife left their home on the 10th of June, carrying only one small suitcase and leaving behind them irreplaceable scores and manuscripts. At the station they had to wait in line for four hours before they could get tickets; and while they were thus occupied, the station gates were closed, shutting out a devoted old friend who had tried to bring Martinů's manuscripts to the train.[1] The story of this friendship is very characteristic of Martinů's comradeship with the common people. The old man was a "bricoleur," a type often found in Paris, who had no regular employment and only worked when he felt like it. But he would have done anything in the world for Martinů, to whom he had attached himself with doglike devotion 'way back in the days when the composer was living in poverty at Montrouge. If ever any little job had to be done, Père Gogo, as they called the old man, would always turn up to do it; he mended Martinů's furniture, helped him when he moved to new quarters, and constituted himself a general handy-man without ever being willing to accept a penny for his services.[2] On this occasion he waited

[1] Some of Martinů's manuscripts were sent to Bordeaux with the intention that an acquaintance of his should bring them to America. But through an unlucky chance the baggage was exchanged with someone else's, and Martinů's suitcase remained in France.

[2] I cannot give his name, because he is most probably still living in France and guarding Martinů's manuscripts.

vainly to deliver the precious scores to their owner; for by sheer chance Martinů, after receiving his railway tickets, had noticed that an unannounced train was on the point of leaving for Limoges. It was entirely empty in spite of the fact that crowds of people were thronging the station waiting for a chance to board any train that would take them away from Paris — a situation typical of the confusion of those days. Feeling that this was too good an opportunity to be missed, even though it meant leaving all their baggage behind, Martinů and his wife boarded the train and left the threatened city.

After an exhausting journey they arrived at Villefavard, near Limoges, where they were welcomed by their friend Charles Munch, who managed to find accommodation for them in an old house in Rancon, a neighboring village. The house was so primitive that their meals had to be cooked over an open fireplace. Martinů's wife, however, had the situation well in hand, and a few hours after their arrival had already organized all the details of their temporary ménage. She also did everything she could to bolster up her husband's low morale. But he did not like Limoges at all. Always, on arriving at a new place, he would look for two things: bookshops and a park in which to take his evening walks. But Limoges boasted only one very inferior bookshop, and when Martinů went there he was shocked at the poor selection of books obtainable. This seemed to him the last straw, when added to his homesickness for Paris and his worry and misery over the whole situation. In the meantime the Germans were only a dozen miles away, and Martinů knew that he must escape as soon as possible. For he was on the Nazi blacklist because he had failed to comply with the order to return to Czechoslovakia, and also because of the help he had given to the Czechoslovak National Council ever since the beginning of the war. He and his wife therefore decided to make an attempt to cross the frontier of

France in secret, and soon set out on foot for the Pyrenees. They were unsuccessful in this undertaking and, worn out by the journey and lack of food, they decided to accept an invitation to stay with some friends in Aix-en-Provence. But even here in the beautiful countryside of southern France they could not rest, for Martinů could still think of nothing but his desire to reach America.

During these uncertain weeks in Provence he wrote a composition for piano, Fantasia and Rondo, dedicated to his friend Rudolf Firkušný, the Czech pianist, who was at that time in Marseille, also preparing to go to America. This was Martinů's first and is still his only important work for piano solo. It was composed in the chaotic time after the defeat of France. Consequently it is a dramatic and complex work, in the same vein as the Double Concerto.

The Martinůs were entirely without any financial means during their stay in Aix-en-Provence, and but for the help of friends would not have had money for even the barest essentials of life. The sum necessary to take them to Lisbon and for the passage to America was completely beyond their reach. In spite of this Martinů now began to make attempts to get an American visa. Again and again he unsuccessfully visited the various passport offices in southern France and finally in desperation turned to his friends in America. When at long last he got the news that he had been granted his visa in a special cable from the State Department to the American Consul in Marseille,[3] he was so overjoyed that he immediately began to write a Sinfonietta Giocosa for piano and chamber orchestra. "I cannot describe with what happiness I received your letter," he wrote to me; "it was truly a message from the New World. . . . Immediately I started with the passport formalities. The American Consul welcomed me warmly; in

---

[3] Through the intervention of the Czechoslovak Minister, Vladimír S. Hurban, in Washington.

three days everything was ready and — thanks to you — we now have our visas for America."

The *Sinfonietta*, dedicated to Germaine Leroux,[4] who has for many years been an exponent of Martinů's music, is highly significant in the development of his work. It is of an unexpected genre, as he himself wrote to Mme Leroux at the time of its completion. The greater part of it was composed in an uncomfortable trolley-car running from Aix-en-Provence to Marseille, where between the middle of October and the middle of November 1940 he had to go almost every day in connection with his visa. He wrote it on the last sheets of music paper obtainable in Marseille; and the score was completed in an absolutely unheated room in Aix-en-Provence. "My hands are numb with cold," he wrote, "but this is not discernible in the music." The work shows Martinů's will to overcome his worries, and is of a joyful, positive, unmistakably Czech nature. All the hardships of this most unhappy period in his life were conquered by music. Although the original plans for the *Sinfonietta* had included a Largo, he now, in the midst of this difficult time, was able to write in no vein other than one of gaiety and happiness. The work is in four movements and they are all Allegro. The customary Andante is replaced in the second movement by a Scherzando in "walking tempo." "I am pleased with my Scherzo," he wrote on October 26; "I have managed to wheedle an unheard-of amount of tone out of the small ensemble, and the Scherzo promises well." The solo piano part is not written in the usual pianistic style but is, rather, worked out in two-part counterpoint supported by an orchestra consisting of flute, two oboes, two bassoons, horn, and strings. It is conceived in a strongly accentuated style, which is further complicated by an occa-

---

[4] Germaine Leroux gave the first performance of the *Sinfonietta Giocosa* in Carnegie Hall in New York on March 16, 1942, with the National Orchestral Association (Leon Barzin, conductor).

sional intentional omission of bar-lines as well as by great rhythmic contrast between the solo part and the orchestra. According to a suggestion written on the score by the composer, it can be played by nineteen or twenty players (six wind instruments, three or four first violins, three second violins, two violas, three cellos, and two double-basses), or alternatively with a larger string section.

It is entirely characteristic of Martinů's psychological reaction to material conditions that even in those troubled days he was trying to find a libretto for a comic opera. For some time he considered *Bal de Voleurs*, by Jean Anouilh, but was obliged to give up the idea on account of the difficulty of making contact with the author, who was still in Paris. "If you know of a suitable comedy by an American writer, do keep it in mind for me," he wrote to friends in America during the last days of 1940. "I want to start working on an opera buffa. I have some original ideas for it." Ever since his *Suburban Theater* Martinů had wished to write another comic opera, and to this day is still occupied with the idea.

He was still waiting, in spite of the special visa presented to him in Marseille,[5] to complete the final arrangements for his journey to America. For at the end of October, just as he was putting the last touches to the second movement of the *Sinfonietta*, the Vichy Government — giving no specific reason — refused to issue him an exit permit.[6] Only after considerable pressure on the part of Martinů's friends in America, assisted by the League of Composers and Miss Dorothy Lawton (secretary of the International Society of Contemporary Music), did the Vichy ambassador in Washington, fearing a scandal, recommend to his Government in France that Martinů's exit permit be granted. In the meanwhile the

---

[5] The State Department described Martinů as an outstanding musician; but the modest composer was greatly embarrassed on being asked by the American Consul in Marseille for proof of this flattering title.

[6] The pianist Alfred Cortot was the head of the Cultural Division at Vichy.

Excambion, on which the composer and his wife had reserved two berths, left Lisbon on Christmas Day. His exit permit had finally arrived in the middle of December, but he was still without the necessary Spanish transit visa. Again his American friends set to work, through a special recommendation from Sir Charles Mendl, but were not able to get it for him till early in January. Then, however, he was able to set his departure for March 21, on the ship *Exeter.*

Financial questions relating to the journey were also the cause of many a sleepless night for the composer. His friends did all they could to help him. The Swiss cellist G. Honegger commissioned a new composition, which Martinů started immediately after the completion of the *Sinfonietta Giocosa.* This work is a *Sonata da Camera* for cello and chamber orchestra, of a serious and dramatic nature, in some ways similar to the *Concerto da Camera* for violin and string orchestra (with piano and tympani) which he wrote in America later in the year. Both works are in the form — basically a concerto grosso — which dominates much of Martinů's work.

A touching tribute was paid to the forsaken composer at this time by some anonymous Swiss admirers of his music. An article appeared in the Swiss paper *Dissonances* appealing for funds for Martinů.[7] The response was excellent, and at last

---

[7] The text of the appeal is here given:

For a Musician in Distress

A foreign composer, whose name — though we naturally cannot make it public on this occasion — is justly considered to be one of the greatest in contemporary music, his works having often been applauded at concerts of the Orchestre Romand as well as in many other cities beyond our borders, finds himself completely destitute, having been obliged to leave Paris (where he made his living for some years), leaving behind him his manuscripts and his few personal belongings.

He and his wife have taken refuge in a small provincial town in France, where they are at the moment enduring the greatest privations.

In view of this undeserved hardship which has so cruelly hit a gifted artist, *Dissonances* wishes to appeal to the generosity of its readers. Even the smallest contribution will be received with the greatest appreciation.

(Revue Musicale Indépendante *Dissonances,* Geneva, No. 6, October 1940. Rédacteur: R. Aloys Mooser.)

he and his wife were in a position to undertake the journey to America, for which the Swiss conductor Paul Sacher bought the steamship tickets. He arrived in Lisbon about the middle of January 1941 — an abnormally thin, tall, worried man, in whom his friends would hardly have recognized the former youthful-looking Bohuslav Martinů. His devoted wife was with him. But their sailing, set for February 15, had to be postponed again, and a wait of nearly three long months still stretched before them, to be spent in an environment that might have been one of Goya's paintings of poor Europe. "I am not doing anything; I'm terribly bored and can't even rest," Martinů wrote. For him, resting means activity, but activity under happy conditions; inactivity is disastrous to him. "I should like to stand on a more solid base," he continues; "this life of eternal waiting, without knowing why or for how long, does not suit me; and the waste of time gets on my nerves. I want to start work again."

15 : In America

ON March 27 Martinů wirelessed from the S.S. *Exeter*: "Arrivons Exeter lundi 31 Mars Venez au bateau amitiés Martinů." And on the morning of March 31, as the ship began to draw near the New Jersey pier, the tall figure of the new immigrant could clearly be seen standing on the deck. He had changed tremendously. His thin figure, haggard face, and sad eyes, in which only occasionally a spark of joy appeared, showed what suffering he had gone through since the autumn of 1938. There were still a few formalities on landing, and after that Martinů, with his wife and their modest baggage, was taken to a midtown New York hotel. Here he was heartily welcomed by friends, as well as by others who knew him only by name. A reception, arranged through the American composer Frederick Jacobi, was given by Mrs. Arthur M. Reis and the League of Composers, and was attended by many musicians. Martinů was terribly tired, but new impressions and the hope of being able to work again helped him to recuperate. He missed his long quiet evening walks, however. "Walking alone at night helps me to relax," he explained.[1] "Sometimes in this way I can work out problems of composition that have worried me for days. That is why I like to walk alone." While in New York he wrote a Mazurka for piano for the Paderewski Memorial — his first composition produced on American soil. He longed for the country, however, and towards the middle of June left for Pleasantville, New York, to stay with the same friends with whom he had spent the first few months in New York. Here he rested in peaceful surroundings and revised his Sinfonietta Giocosa. Later he went to Edgartown, Massachusetts, where he lived in the artists' colony.[2] By this time his health had much improved. From Switzerland he got a cable from Paul Sacher, with a request for a new violin concerto, which the conductor planned to perform in January of the following year, together with Honegger's Symphony for Strings. "Switzerland seems to be the only place in Europe where plans can be made so far ahead," remarked Martinů.

At the beginning of July he started to work with new enthusiasm, and wrote the Concerto da Camera in F minor for solo violin accompanied by string orchestra, piano and tympani. He wished this composition to be an expression of gratitude to his friends in Switzerland, and sent it off to Basel,

---

[1] In the Long Island Daily Press, January 31, 1942.
[2] Also staying there were Bernard Wagenaar and Leopold Mannes, who took friendly care of Martinů.

MARTINŮ IN 1922

MARTINŮ ARRIVING IN NEW YORK

where it was duly performed in January 1942. It is a dramatic work of Czech character with a virtuoso part for the solo violin, and is — as has already been pointed out — in the same category as his *Sonata da Camera* for cello and chamber orchestra. The first movement (Moderato, Poco Allegro, 6–8) is in variation form, the solo part presenting the theme in ever quickening tempo, with a vigorous accompaniment in the orchestra. The entire second movement (Adagio, 6–4) is an aria — a single melody throughout. Here the polyphony is more elegant than is usual with Martinů.

The third movement (Poco Allegro, 3–4), thematically related to the first, is in rondo form, with a cadenza consisting of a simple melody accompanied by repeated chords on the piano — very different from the usual virtuoso cadenza.

After a long vacation Martinů settled down to work in Jamaica, Long Island. There during the last months of 1941 he wrote his Second Sonata for cello and piano and revised and completed the *Suite Concertante* for violin and orchestra, which he had begun long before in France and the score of which was already in America in the hands of Samuel Dushkin, to whom it is dedicated. Meanwhile, whenever he had an odd moment he would work at some little songs on folk texts that he had tucked away in his desk drawer. These songs are very characteristic of Martinů and have an important place in his work; they are in no way imitations of folk music, though he composes them in much the same natural and spontaneous manner as that in which such songs originate among the peasants. A collection of these entitled *New Špaliček* was issued to the public in the spring of 1942 [3] and was soon followed by seven songs produced in 1943, under the title *Songs on One Page*.

---

[3] Performed for the first time by Jarmila Novotná, with comments by Olin Downes, at a concert of the Junior League Club in New York, on January 11, 1943.

These songs, as well as their echoes in many of Martinů's other compositions, prove without a doubt that the deepest inspiration of his music is to be found in the soul of the Czechoslovak people. As far as melody and sometimes even harmony are concerned, its source is in the Moravian folksongs. The rhythm is drawn from the Czech and Slovak tradition, but the Moravian influence is the stronger of the two. The region called Moravian Slovakia, southeast of Moravia, has produced folk-songs which are rhythmically and melodically so pure and so original that it is almost impossible to set them down within the confines of regular bars or the current tonal system; and for this reason they have often been inexactly transcribed. Perhaps only Leoš Janáček — in, for instance, his famous opera *Jenufa* — has succeeded in catching the spirit of these curiously "out-of-tune" melodies and changing rhythms. Martinů has been equally fortunate in his treatment of the Moravian folk music. "He never borrows popular tunes, but is constantly indebted to them," said P. O. Ferroud in the *Chesterian*. The slow movements of his recent works, in particular those of the Second Symphony and the Concerto for two pianos, are strongly influenced by these songs, which he, so to speak, re-created in the two books above mentioned. There are many more somewhere in France; about fifty were kept by his pupil Vítězslava Kaprálová, the gifted Czech woman composer. Martinů has already used some texts from these in his ballet *Špalíček* and the opera *The Miracle of Our Lady*. One of the best examples is the song in the scene of "Sister Pascaline" (of which the text is reproduced on pages 58 and 59). It is to be noted that this ends on the dominant, giving an impression of something without end.

If Martinů's creative tendencies could be summarized, one might say that the two pillars upon which his work rests are the form of the concerto grosso and the melody of Czechoslovakia.⁴ These two influences — on the one hand the classic and on the other the popular Slav — are fused in his work. This important fact clearly indicates his Czech character, since the traditions of the Czechoslovak people have for more than a thousand years combined the Byzantine element with the culture of the Western world. In the field of music this is proved by old documents of the liturgic chants of the ninth century, coming from the period of the Great Moravian Empire — the first Slav empire in the history of the world — which engulfed, among other places, the territory of modern Czechoslovakia.⁵ The Czech musicologist Professor D. Orel, of the Comenius University of Bratislava, has brought forward the theory that the development of the ancient Czech liturgic chant is altogether independent of any influence of neighboring countries. This is also the case with Czech architecture of the tenth and eleventh centuries, as well as with the Slav alphabet used by the church even before that time.

Martinů invariably corrects people who think he comes from Bohemia. "Yes," he says, "I do; but ethnologically Polička belongs to Moravia." His songs are simple and direct, just like the Czechoslovak folklore, which originates from a matter-of-

⁴ Something of the same kind is now happening in Soviet Russia. By a happy chance I recently had the opportunity — through a courtesy of Miss Helen Black, American representative of the Literary Service of the USSR — to read the manuscript of a new book, *Modern Musical Thought*, by the outstanding Soviet musicologist A. S. Ogolovets. This gives many definite answers to fundamental questions concerning old music, and is a large and important contribution to the science of melody and harmony based on studies of Oriental folk music. The chapter on the development of the tonal system is particularly ingenious. Ogolovets, though he holds classical music in high esteem, is critical of the music and musical thought of the nineteenth century. He sees new possibilities for contemporary composers, however, in the study of folk music, which he believes to contain the essence of musical art. It is encouraging to see that a Soviet writer says: "Not all new things are signs of progress." This book, the result of thirty years of research, is, as Dmitri Shostakovich rightly says in the introduction: "An enormous step forward in the world literature of music, and opens broad perspectives before the theoreticians of music, its historians, and also the composers."

⁵ See the book *Wisdom of the Old Czechs*, by Roman Jakobson, published in Czech by the Czechoslovak Cultural Circle in New York in 1943.

fact people. But they also contain the Czech dignity and nobility.[6]

In the spring of 1942 Martinů wrote his First Piano Quartet, originally intended for the jubilee of the League of Composers. In this work he integrates Czechoslovak melodic material into a highly musical form; and, as is evident from the following example, the style is extremely polyphonic:

The Piano Quartet was first performed at the Berkshire Music Center in Lenox, Massachusetts, and made a great impression upon the listeners, of whom the majority were musicians.

16 : The First Symphony

AFTER the success of the *Concerto Grosso*, Martinů began to make preparations for an important work, the First Symphony, commissioned by the Koussevitzky Music Foundation. As has been said before, he had, with one or two

---

[6] I use here the classification of folk music by Sir C. Hubert H. Parry in his book *The Evolution of the Art of Music*.

MARTINŮ WITH KOUSSEVITZKY

CHARLOTTE MARTINŮ, THE
COMPOSER'S WIFE

exceptions, written almost nothing for large orchestra since *La Rhapsodie* in 1928. For nearly fourteen years he had been engrossed in composing for chamber orchestra; and a full-size symphony raised new problems, not only technically, but also because of the great importance that this form held for him. The commission of the Koussevitzky Foundation called for an orchestral composition in any form the composer might choose. So it was Martinů himself who decided upon a symphony. He had just passed his fiftieth year, and had produced over a hundred compositions. Up to this time, however, he had not tried his hand at a symphony. After some hesitation he began to work on the first movement. He was then in Jamaica, Long Island, but in the middle of June 1942 left for Middlebury, Vermont, where it took him some days to settle down. He had to search the town for a piano, and on finally finding one discovered it was almost too large to move into his small room.

Just at this time a telegram from Koussevitzky arrived, offering him the position of professor at the advanced school of composition at the Berkshire Music Center. Martinů accepted, but frankly stressed his meager knowledge of English speech. He was to start his lectures at Tanglewood on the first of July and remain there for six wecks. For the present, however, he was quite happy in Middlebury, enjoying the peace and quiet of Vermont. He was working very hard, for when he moved to the Berkshires he had already written — actually in ten days — the second and third movements of his symphony. The second movement (Scherzo) took him less than a week and was finished on June 26. The fourth movement he composed at Lenox, during his engagement at the Berkshire Music Center. There he shared his pupils with the American composer Aaron Copland, and his lectures on musical style attracted a good deal of attention. The score of the symphony was finally completed on September 1 at Manomet, Massachusetts.[1]

The First Symphony is a landmark in Martinů's work. It is entirely different from the rest of his orchestral compositions while at the same time containing many of his most individual characteristics, particularly as to form. The only earlier work to which it bears any resemblance is the opera *Juliette*, possibly because both are scored for large orchestra. In performance the symphony demands a very exact reading, and here the Boston Symphony Orchestra, under the baton of Serge Koussevitzky, had an opportunity to apply its high standards.[2] The concentration and careful planning with which Martinů wrote this work are evident in his program notes for the Boston concert, in which he voices his basic theories of the problems of form confronting the composer of a modern symphony. These notes contain some of the most significant declarations he has yet made. The text is here given in full:

The form of the symphony is one of the great problems of contemporary composers. The century past has left us a form well established not only in structure but in its content of elevated expression and grandeur. The Ninth Symphony of Beethoven has been an example. The Romantic and post-Romantic epochs have added a further and a very earnest ideology — a sentiment tragic, pathetic, even grandiloquent, have placed the symphony at the highest level of musical composition. It is certainly not my intention to dispute this natural and logical position. I wish only to clarify a certain conviction which

---

[1] While in Manomet the Martinůs, who were living in a small cottage by the sea, became involved in a curious incident. It was just at the time that a coast guard had discovered the landing of Nazi saboteurs at various places on the coast; and Martinů, being a foreigner, was for a time taken to be one of them. Neither the testimony of the owner of the cottage nor that of Emmanuel Ondríček, the well-known violin professor from Boston, was able to convince the zealous coast guard of his mistake. The matter was fortunately cleared up the following day.

[2] The symphony was given its first performance on November 13, 1942 in Boston, and its second and third performances in New York on November 21 and January 7. It was also on a Boston Symphony program in New Haven, Connecticut, but owing to a black-out only the first movement could be played.

has resulted from the development of the form in our time. In spite of several attempts of contemporary composers to change the structure, to find another solution in writing a symphony in a single movement, in five parts, etc., its essential nature remains unchanged, with rare exceptions. There enter here the problems which disturb the composer when he begins a work and when he assembles his musical, ideological and technical material.

To forestall misinterpretation of my remarks and to avoid seeming dogmatic, I should like to offer as my own the thoughts and sentiments with which I have undertaken the present work. The large proportions, the expansive form of the symphony necessarily force the composer to put himself on a high plane. The concept of elevated thought is certainly incontestable, the question really becoming what we consider elevated thought to be. What I maintain as my deepest conviction is the essential nobility of thoughts and things which are quite simple and which, not explained in high-sounding words and abstruse phrases, still hold an ethical and human significance. It is possible that my thoughts dwell upon objects or events of an almost everyday simplicity familiar to everyone and not exclusively to certain great spirits. They may be so simple as to pass almost unnoticed but may still contain a deep meaning and afford great pleasure to humanity, which, without them, would find life pale and flat. It could also be that these things permit us to go through life more easily, and, if one gives them due place, touch the highest plane of thought. One must also recognize the truth that a work so great and weighty as the Ninth Symphony of Beethoven could have been conceived only at a certain moment in history with the concurrence of certain conditions, and could not have been written just by any one and just at any time. A different point of view could falsify creative activity at the start, and could force the composer into a tragic and pathetic attitude, which would result in nothing else than a "tour de force." It is possible a priori for intended tragedy and pathos to be not tragic at all, and every composer must be wary of false magnitude. Each composer and each creator of our epoch feels himself, to a certain extent, obligated to espouse sentiments of grandeur and tragedy. But this is natural human feeling.[3] I have long pondered over the question, and should like here

---

[3] Owing to a faulty translation from the French in which these notes were originally written a regrettable error appeared in the Boston Symphony program. This passage was made to read: "But this is *no* natural human feeling." The same mistake occurred in my own article in the *Musical Quarterly* of July 1943.

to note its consequences upon the course of music. The tendency, the desire to be greater than one is, can lead directly to an emphasis which, to say the least, is not essentially musical. Overemphasis can certainly strain the limits of music and sound, and by sound I mean dynamics. One inevitably comes to the point where the actual instruments can no longer support the weight of an expression which exaggerates dynamism; they cannot support this expression and still keep faith with certain æsthetic laws which we rightly prize. Even the natural capacity of our ears and nerves is strained. There is still another grave consequence which dynamics conceal: the tendency to mask a lack of real music and to replace it with noise. The result adds nothing to the true beauty of the art, for the sheer excitation of the nerves cannot be the just æsthetic goal. I am aware that this way of expression has its admirers, but I am not thereby convinced that this is the true realm of music, for my aim is something very different. I know, too, that that is the way of many in our own epoch, but neither can this justify for me the use of noise in music. Sheer orchestral power does not necessarily imply either grandeur or elevation.

If we look at the question from the point of view of technique, the consequences are characteristic. This dynamic urge necessarily displaces the balance of the basic function in the orchestra. The strings, which have traditionally furnished the basic element, can no longer do so, their fortissimo sonority being covered when the composer leans heavily upon the brass and percussion. In this way the whole conception of a work becomes "brass," while we lose the charm, the amiability, even the passion, of the stringed instruments and their great variety of expression. We are aroused but not exactly happy, and that we must leave a concert in a state of fatigue is in itself not a favorable sign.

As for my symphony, it follows the classical division into four parts — Allegro, Scherzo, Largo, Allegro. In preserving this plan, I have also followed an æsthetic plan which my conviction dictates, and this conviction is that a work of art must not transcend the limits of its possibility in expression. I lived in France long enough to learn what is the significance of *mesure*.[4] I have avoided elements which seem to me alien to the expressive purpose of the work. The basis of the orchestra is in the quintet of the strings, which does not prevent solo passages

---

[4] The French term *mesure* means a sense of proportion or balance, and was incorrectly translated in the program notes of the Boston Symphony by the word "measure."

for the woodwinds, while the brass and percussion fulfill their due part. I have tried to find new sound combinations and to elicit from the orchestra a unified sonority in spite of the polyphonic working which the score contains. It is not the sonority of impressionism, nor is there the search for color, which rather is integral in the writing and the formal structure. The character of the work is calm and lyric.

This is an authoritative statement. We may add that the principles it expresses are entirely realized in the work itself. Virgil Thomson, who heard the symphony for the first time in New York and did not know Martinů's thesis, wrote as follows: [5]

The Martinů Symphony is a beaut. It is wholly lovely and doesn't sound like anything else . . . the shining sounds of it sing as well as shine; the instrumental complication is a part of the musical conception, not an icing laid over it. Personal indeed is the delicate but vigorous rhythmic animation, the singing (rather than dynamic) syncopation that permeates the work. Personal and individual, too, is the whole orchestral sound of it, the acoustical superstructure that shimmers consistently.

The following example from the First Symphony shows Martinů's delight in freeing phrases from any dependence upon the regularity of the bar:

Poco Allegro:

The structure of the symphony, despite the many interesting color effects it contains, is firm and uniform throughout. "You could not change one note in this work. It is like a classical symphony," said Koussevitzky. The first movement (6–8) opens with a chord of B minor, which is taken up by glittering chromatic scales on the strings, harp, and piano, changing it to B major and introducing the spacious horizon of the com-

[5] In the *New York Herald Tribune*, November 22, 1942.

position. The strings carry on the subject, which appears again in exulting major harmony in the brass towards the end of the movement. As is Martinů's way, this is reached without a climax, and is framed by chords from the beginning of the symphony. The second movement, a Scherzo of Czech character, is rhythmical and richly varied, with a trio which seems to soothe the dancing tempo of the jubilant orchestra. In the third movement a broad and noble melody is unfolded by the strings. The fourth movement is particularly interesting; it gives the effect of chamber music, its jovial character forming a contrast to the Scherzo of the second movement because of a series of melodic ideas of which the last, in the wit and freshness of its motive, is almost reminiscent of Mozart. It is very Czech, however, very positive. In structure the entire work is well proportioned, and its form, though it deviates from the customary sonata form, is firmly maintained.

17 : The Second Symphony

EVEN while completely absorbed in the composition of the First Symphony in the summer of 1942, Martinů knew that he would soon write a second; he was fascinated by the sonority that a large orchestra is capable of producing. The First Symphony glows in tonal colors; in the words of Virgil Thomson, "the orchestra shimmers in all its beauty." Martinů had in mind a second symphony which should be written for large orchestra, but conceived in chamber-music style in order to enable him to work with small solo groups. This plan materialized exactly a year later. He began, however, by writing an Allegro in the form of a march for full orchestra — another example of the way his inspiration of the

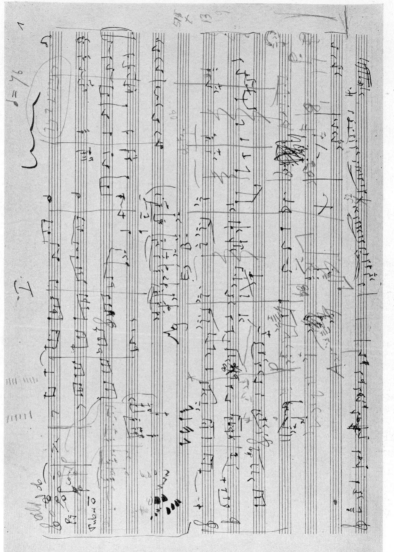

THE SECOND SYMPHONY (OPENING) IN SKETCH

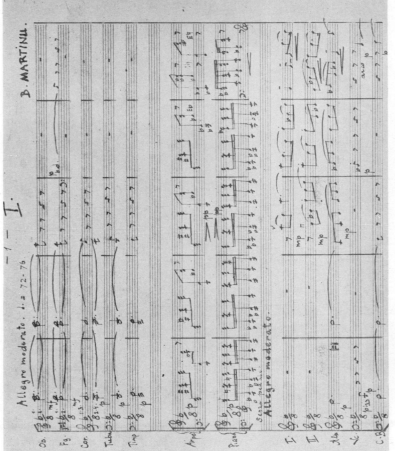

THE SECOND SYMPHONY (OPENING) IN SCORE

moment is liable to thwart his preconceived plans. Nevertheless he returned to his original idea of a chamber-music symphony for full orchestra. Simply laying aside the first six pages of this Allegro, intending ultimately to use them in the third movement, he began a fresh first movement (Allegro moderato, 6–8). The Second Symphony opens with a D-minor chord, sustained on the wind instruments and lower strings, with accompaniment of piano and harp. The reader can find this on the next two pages in the original sketch, as well as in the completed score. Comparison of the two shows clearly the cryptic notes that are all Martinů needs in order to transcribe the final manuscript of the score directly onto the master sheet with indelible ink. This particular sketch is more confused than some others in which only the main theme and a few notes of the orchestration are indicated. The small short lines on either side of the sketch and the numbers on the right-hand side show the number of staves which will be needed for this page in the definitive manuscript.

Any attempt to explain the piano and harp accompaniment in a programmatic way would be a grave mistake. Actually it is merely the following almost Mozartian figure:

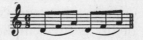

The main theme, of a calm and pastoral nature, appears in the third bar. It is introduced by violins and violas, with a simple pizzicato accompaniment on the cellos and basses, but is soon taken over by a group of woodwinds accompanied by muted strings. Before long a motive in sixteenth notes is introduced; this is not so much a second subject as a sort of filling-in passage, which appears again towards the end of the movement. It is only used in the recapitulation, where it accompanies variations on the main theme without ever reaching a climax.

The second movement (Andante) has the character of a Moravian folk-song, almost in the style of Janáček. It starts on the oboe and clarinet, with sustained notes on the violas.

The melody is soon taken up in a more developed form by the other strings. The whole movement, during which the woodwind and strings play alternately, is in a pastoral mood.

Another example from this slow movement shows some of Martinů's characteristic harmonic and melodic craftsmanship:

As aforementioned, the third movement (Scherzando) is the march from the original score, and contains some of the most striking music of the entire symphony; and here Martinů employs the full orchestra. Only at the end of the movement does the scoring become simpler and calmer in feeling, with a suggestion of the *Marseillaise* on the trumpets leading back to the original march.

This is a typical instance of Martinů's rhythmic originality:

The opening of the fourth movement is of a neutral nature, being intended as a bridge between the mood of the march and the Finale proper, which is written in rondo form. In sonority it has some resemblance to the second movement. The main subject is again based on a sixteenth-note pattern of classical character, almost identical with the second theme of the first movement. This is followed by a simple melody, rather like a Moravian folk-song, introduced by the oboe and bassoon to a unique string accompaniment that is comparable only to the sound of the rustling of leaves on the trees. The tune shifts to the cellos and then, in typical rondo form, is developed on all the strings. In the Coda the sixteenth-note motive reappears, and the main theme of the first movement — transposed to D major — is combined with the folk melody.

As a whole, the Second Symphony is a typically Czech work — the result of long preparation, felicitous ideas, and successful working out. It is pastoral in feeling, practically classical in form, and shaped by the composer's inspiration rather than by any conscious intention on his part. The dedication: "To my Fellow-Countrymen in Cleveland" is particularly interesting, for it was collectively commissioned by a group of American citizens of Czechoslovak extraction living in Cleveland who, as the *Cleveland Press* put it, "have contributed so much to the industrial and cultural life of the city, and of whom the majority are workers in the common cause of the war effort." [1] In spite of this the symphony is far from being of a popular or utilitarian character. It has an almost Mozartian simplicity and does not contain one note of artistic compromise. Mar-

---

[1] The Second Symphony was performed for the first time in Cleveland on October 28 and 30, 1943 — the Independence Day of Czechoslovakia, and the twenty-fifth anniversary of the founding of the Czechoslovakian Republic — by the Cleveland Orchestra under Erich Leinsdorf; and for the second time in New York on December 30 and 31, 1943 and January 1, 1944, by the New York Philharmonic Orchestra conducted by Artur Rodzinski.

tinů's theories are in complete contradiction to Marx's materialistic philosophy of art. The fact that the Second Symphony was enthusiastically applauded by the workers of Cleveland is only one more example of the immediate response his music arouses among people in the mass.

The notes prepared by Martinů for the Cleveland program are as follows:

The statement that I made when my First Symphony was introduced in Boston is also applicable to my Second Symphony.

We have seen how the form of the symphony began to spread out, to grow larger and to assume the greatest length and breadth from Beethoven's time up to the period of Bruckner and Mahler. In contemporary hands, the symphony has returned to older, more reasonable proportions, but the form and the content are always thought of as the expression of something grandiose, tragic or pathetic, in a certain sense dependent upon a "program"; in other words, the idea remains literary rather than musical. As I have already written above, difficulties and complications present themselves when a composer is trying to express elevated thoughts, and I have also pointed out that simple events and simple things may appear "grandiose" to the artist. In themselves they may not seem so spectacular, but in music they may become quite as spectacular and just as inspiring.

We come now to the problem of musical expression, to the fact that composers have not yet discovered the means of expressing the grand and the tragic within purely musical limits, and have gone beyond them by mechanical means and dynamic design, ending simply in noise, which, with the best will in the world, cannot be considered in the domain of music. I am not speaking against the proper use of intensity to realize a musical idea; I have used it very often in my works. But I do object to the employment in music of noise produced mechanically with the help of open-air instruments, the effect of which, I admit, is irresistible, but which react upon the nerves alone. Such a reaction is not the purpose of music and beauty. No sincere musician will make it his ideal to destroy the nerves of his listeners. The result is negative, not positive.

Of course, I don't mean to rule out the dramatic conception of a musical work. My Second Symphony, the case in point, is calm and lyric. It seems to me that we have no need of a professional and technical expression of torture; rather do we need orderly thought, expressed calmly.

I have given up analyzing my works in detail. A composition is a whole and the public should listen to it as a whole. To follow such details as motive, subject, counter-subject, development, etc., doesn't help very much, and explains nothing. They are so evident that it is not worth while to make a new story about them. Such analysis is a kind of puzzle; it is not as a puzzle that I have composed the symphony; and I don't want people to listen to it as a puzzle.

A charming incident of the Cleveland concert was the presentation to Martinů of enormous baskets of flowers brought on the stage by young girls in Czech costume. The whole town was in a state of excitement a week before the occasion, and the *Cleveland Plain Dealer* published an editorial entitled: "Czechoslovakia Still Sings." It reads: "Any people who can sing under adversity as they sang last night in the stirring melodies of the Martinů Symphony are freedom's destined children."

18 : The Violin Concerto and Other Works

As has been the case with several of Martinů's compositions, the Violin Concerto was undertaken by sheer chance. At the beginning of January 1943 the violinist Mischa Elman, wishing to hear the Seventh Symphony of Shostakovich, attended a concert given in Carnegie Hall by the Boston Symphony Orchestra under Serge Koussevitzky. He had mistaken the date, however, and instead of the Shostakovich the First Symphony of Martinů was on the program. Though not particularly interested beforehand, Elman ended by being so entirely captivated by Martinů's music that he visited the composer the following day and then and there commissioned him to write a violin concerto. The two artists had never met before, and at first found it somewhat difficult to understand each other. Martinů's monosyllabic manner was puzzling to Elman, who tried to break the ice by inquiring if he had heard any of the living world-famous violinists. "No," was the reply. "Are you by any chance familiar with my playing?" ventured Elman. "No," said Martinů flatly. There was a prolonged silence. Finally Elman tried to solve the problem by taking Martinů to his studio and playing to him for half an hour or so. The composer listened very attentively, though with complete impassivity. After the last note Elman, very naturally, stood and waited for his reaction. But Martinů continued to sit in sphinx-like silence, which remained unbroken until he got up to leave and the two musicians bade each other an awkward good-bye. The violinist was completely baffled, and feared his scheme must result in failure. Before long, however, Martinů duly appeared with the finished score of a new violin concerto and it did not take Elman long to recognize that the work had been written specially for him and his personal style, and would give him an excellent opportunity for the expression of all his fine technical and emotional qualities. At Elman's suggestion, Martinů added a cadenza at the end of the first part. The manuscript of the score bears the dedication "To Misha [sic] Elman," and the title in French: "Concert p. violon."

While Martinů was at work on this concerto I once asked him what its nature was. "Violin," replied Martinů briefly. And it is a fact that this composition sums up with infallible insight the indefinable emotional appeal of the instrument, making it sing in its true manner of expression. Although the concerto is a modern work, the treatment of the violin technique — which has remained unchanged for so many years — is on classical lines.

Martinů wrote for the Boston Symphony Orchestra program the following notes about the concerto and the problems with which he was confronted while writing it:

The idea for this concerto presented itself to me with the following order — *Andante*, a broad lyric song of great intensity which leads to an *Allegro* exploiting the technique and the virtuosity of the instrument, and has the aspect of a single-movement composition. The definitive form complies with concerto structure. I have preserved its grave character, lyric in the first part; and even in the middle *Allegro* the *Andante* theme returns to end the movement. The second part is a sort of point of rest, a bridge progressing towards the *Allegro* finale. It is an *Intermezzo moderato*, almost bucolic, accompanied by only a part of the orchestra and progressing *attacca* into the finale, which is *Allegro*. This favors the technique of the violin, which is interrupted by broad and massive *"tutti"* passages. The concerto ends with a sort of *"stretto," Allegro vivo*.

I should like to add a few points which came to me as I composed it and which might throw a little light on that most difficult problem — writing a violin concerto. As with all compositions for solo instrument, the solo violin requires a quite special "state of mind." A piano solo allows us to preserve the image of the musical thought in its full scope, that is to say, almost complete with harmony, polyphony, color and the dynamics of orchestral structure. For the violin solo, all which we wish to express must be contained in a single line, which must also imply the rest. To put it differently, the single part of the violin solo must in itself already contain the whole musical scheme, the whole concerto. We have in musical literature certain types of violin concertos which I could define as concertos which exploit beauty of tone against an orchestral background (as in Mozart), or a concerto which exploits the sonority of the solo instrument together with the orchestra; there are also those where the violin is exploited from a professional point of view without much originality of composition. Finally, there are those concertos in which one exploits the orchestra and adds a violin solo, without paying too much attention to its inherent tonal beauties. It is at this point that the problem becomes confused. In working with the orchestra we have lost the capacity of "thinking solo." We become accustomed to having at our disposal the variegated possibilities of the orchestra, which more often than not become an inducement to "express something"; that is to say, the emotional elements, inevitably tending toward intensity of accent and dynamics, result in a confusion as these elements serve to intensify not the real musical content but the dynamics of tone, sound and power. This we can do with an orchestra, but we cannot do it so easily with a solo instrument, least of all with a violin solo. A melody whose structure fulfills the function of a string orchestra is not necessarily a melody which will be adequate for the violin solo. The dynamics, nuances, and the difference between *p-mf-f* of the violin solo are limited and in no way comparable to the dynamic power of the string orchestra. In short, we confound a single violin with a group of violins, with a resulting conflict between desire and ability. It is just here that a composition requires a different state of mind for its whole structure and for the content of the musical idea. Here the motivation of the actual music — dynamic, romantic — cannot help us much. We find ourselves before an old problem of music as music, "absolute music," as against expressive music (in the literary sense of expressing "something"). But this is a problem where misunderstanding so often arises from the confusion of "words." My only wish has been to touch upon one of the questions which is bound to occupy a composer when he undertakes a violin concerto, and it is not to be assumed from what I have said that I have solved this problem in my composition. I am far from making any such pretension. My wish was to draw attention to this question which has filled my thoughts, and the thoughts of many others, during composition.

The concerto is in symphonic style throughout, as is shown by the following example:

The second movement (Poco Moderato) is in the nature of chamber music — a pastoral intermezzo — and the third movement (Poco Allegro) is of highly virtuoso character.

Just before the composition of the Violin Concerto Martinů wrote his Concerto for two pianos and orchestra, completing it in a very short space of time — between January 3 and February 23, 1943. In this work he takes fullest advantage of all the sonorous and contrapuntal possibilities inherent in such a combination.

"I have used the pianos for the first time in the purely 'solo' sense, with the orchestra as accompaniment," Martinů wrote in the program of the Philadelphia Orchestra. "The form is free; it leans rather toward the Concerto grosso. It demands virtuosity, brilliant piano technique and the timbre of the same two instruments calls forth new colors and new sonorities." The orchestra is not large — two of each wind instrument, strings, timpani, and cymbals. The concerto is in three movements, and is of a predominantly rhythmical nature. The first (Allegro non troppo) contains many ingenious and colorful effects in the combination of the orchestra with the two pianos. The second movement (Adagio), which is without any time signature, is more poetic in character, and includes cadenzas for both pianos. The last movement is a brilliant Rondo in dance rhythm.[1]

Two chamber works were written between the composition of the First Symphony and the Concerto for two pianos. One of these, Variations on a Theme by Rossini for cello and piano, is the first of a series undertaken in consultation with Gregor Piatigorsky, who is interested in a plan for providing a new and important repertoire for the cello.[2] The other is a Madrigal Sonata for flute, violin, and piano, which was written in New York City in November 1942 and first performed at the jubilee concert of the League of Composers on December 9,

---

[1] The Concerto for two pianos was first played on November 5, 6, and 8, 1943, in Philadelphia, by Luboschutz and Nemenoff and the Philadelphia Orchestra under Eugene Ormandy; and on November 9 in New York.

[2] Piatigorsky played the Variations for the first time in New York on May 1, 1943, and again in Town Hall on October 30 of the same year.

1942, in New York. As the title indicates, it is larger than a madrigal, though written in madrigal form. Those familiar with Martinů's music can see in it several points of resemblance with his great Trio for piano, violin, and cello written twelve years earlier, the chief difference between the two being that the Madrigal Sonata is of a more simple and human character. Though in three movements it is actually in two main sections, each of which is a pastorale.

Soon after the completion of the Second Symphony Martinů wrote a short work for full orchestra, *Memorial to Lidice*. This owes its existence to the League of Composers, who asked several composers to give musical expression to some particular incident in the history of this war. Lidice is to the Czechoslovaks — as indeed to the whole civilized world — a symbol of the martyrdom of their nation under Nazi tyranny. Martinů, however, felt that in his case the realization of such a work must depend upon a non-programmatical interpretation. He completed *Memorial to Lidice* in a very short time, during August 1943, in Darien, Connecticut, in preparation for a concert of Czechoslovak music given on the anniversary of the founding of the Czechoslovak Republic.[3] He regards this piece as part of a triptych in concerto-grosso style, of which the first and third movements are to be quick and rhythmic, in contrast to the Largo of the *Memorial*. The title of one of these will probably be *RAF*.

Memorial to Lidice, as a New York critic stated after the première, is "not far from its author's best work."[4] Also, "it is a chant and prayer, sombre but not depressed in mood, aglow with restrained feeling, steady and strong in spirit."[5]

On returning to New York after his 1943 summer in Darien,

---

[3] Given in New York in Carnegie Hall on October 28, 29, and 31, by the New York Philharmonic Symphony, conducted by Artur Rodzinski, and in Philadelphia on December 3, 1943, by the Philadelphia Orchestra under Eugene Ormandy.

[4] *New York Herald Tribune*, October 29, 1943.

[5] Oscar Thompson in the *Sun*, October 29, 1943.

Martinů was absorbed in preparations for three forthcoming premières. During the two weeks between October 28 and November 9 eleven performances of his works were given in New York, Philadelphia, and Cleveland alone. He was present at several of these and was able to witness the enthusiasm of the public. His reaction to such successes is only momentary, however, and on the day after the last of these concerts he was already sitting at his piano at work on a new composition, *Madrigal Stanzas* for violin and piano. These five short pieces show his inclination towards a simple and direct form, springing from his love of sixteenth-century poetry and music. The *Madrigal Stanzas* are all — with the exception of one slow movement — in moderate tempo. The free polyphony which he has developed so highly is here somewhat restricted by the repetition of the themes in each piece. In this series, which is dedicated to the famous scientist Albert Einstein, Martinů pays homage to the discoverer of the theory of relativity, as well as to science in general. Knowing that Einstein is a good amateur violinist, he has written the pieces in a style which makes them not too difficult for amateur players.

Since his arrival in America there has been no relaxation of Martinů's efforts in composition; indeed, he has so many plans in mind for the future that before this book is in print there will doubtless be many new additions to the already extraordinary long list of his works.

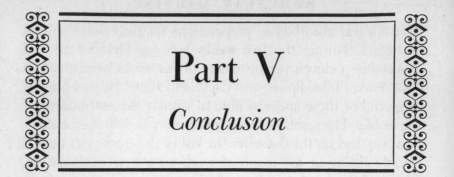

Part V
Conclusion

19 : Martinů's Creative Process

si nemo exquaerat, scio:
si quarenti explicari velim nescio
Saint Augustine: *Confessions*, XI

ONE of the prerequisites for artistic creation is the ability to concentrate — not only consciously and deliberately, but also by a subconscious absorption in abstract impulses. From a logical point of view the act of concentration is a conscious one; in reality, however, this is not always the case, since the conception of a new idea is often the direct result of an inception which cannot be defined or described with precision. In the case of music the composer may even at first be completely in the dark as to how it will ultimately be expressed in notes. But the idea forces itself relentlessly upon him, with a strong urge towards completion. It is at first merely a nebulous sensation, indefinite and uncontrollable. But it can become very persistent without the composer himself being fully aware of its nature and significance; and a great deal depends upon his power to grasp and focus it. With Martinů this intangible feeling often assumes an almost plastic quality, though he is unable to define its shape or dimensions. It is, so to speak, the sensation of an object which can be touched by the imagination; the anticipation of a whole. Perhaps the best comparison might be found in the viewing of a wide countryside: our vision takes in the scene as a whole, but we cannot define it with exactness unless we concentrate on individual details. Once we are aware of these details, however, we are able to reconstruct the entire panorama and retain it in memory. It is detail that first attracts our attention. Although our sweep of vision embraces the entire countryside, only that part of it upon which we concentrate our attention is actually visible, the remainder being surmised by the aid of habit, memory, and experience.

Thus the question arises whether it is possible to take in an impression as a whole or whether we assemble it mentally from its individual components. Actually, this grasp of the whole is one of the fundamentals of all artistic effort. It does not, however, in any way indicate to a composer in what form his work will be written, or what its nature will be. It also does not necessarily result in an immediate capture of the right motive. There are many cases in which a composer finds it necessary to change a motive completely or even to discard it for a new one, as is shown by the notes in Beethoven's sketchbooks. The reason for these alterations is that the motive is not always found to satisfy the requirements of the composition as a whole. Sometimes, however, some very slight change of key or rhythm or even, in the case of vocal music, of the text, may bring the motive into alignment with the composer's general idea. And this almost indefinable conception calls for a quite particular type of concentration and experience. It is in no way the outcome of any concrete search. It is possible to look for a thing one needs if one is familiar with it; but one cannot look for something if one does not know what it is. The search consists, rather, in a certain probing, a certain stabilizing of ideas which approximately correspond with one's vision. Even then the difficulty is to find motives that correspond to the vision as a whole; for at this stage the artist is unable to tell whether they satisfy his conception, since the conception itself is still undefined. It is a feeling of direction, and the motive but a detail. Therefore the purpose of concentration should be to apprehend the objective from every possible angle simultaneously.

This does not mean, as is the popular idea, that a composer is visited by an ecstatic inspiration, in which he hears inaudible music played on invisible harps by unseen hands. On the contrary, it means that something has to be painfully forced from the very core of his consciousness — something that wishes to live and that only he can bring to life. Far from being a poetic or ceremonial act or a state of exalted contemplation, it is a struggle to give birth to an idea which the composer, by hard human labor, is trying to express in his very own way. In a similar manner a scientist grapples with a new discovery or a philosopher with a new principle.

Once this conception of the whole has begun to enter the artist's consciousness, he is able to take the work firmly in hand, not only as regards structure but also emotionally; and from that time on, no outside conditions or reactions resulting from other sources will be able to disturb him. After all, the emotional complex of a man changes continually, and even very strong feelings do not always last long either in actuality or in memory. But the fundamental emotions which shape the will of the artist, and differ so greatly from those coming from outside, remain constant in one direction. In other words, they cease to be simply emotions and become a state of mind which, although to a certain extent also emotional, is in a completely different category.

Thus the composer arrives at the moment which is commonly called inspiration, but which in truth is something far more mysterious. It is in reality the result of a subconscious process of thought, allied to real hard work and a kind of alignment of direction, rather than a vision from heaven. It is also often a matter of relaxation. For instance, a composer may find on getting up in the morning that an idea he had tediously and vainly sought the day before has subconsciously crystallized overnight. It is of course true that inspiration can be evoked by some strong emotion coming from outside; but in actuality this has nothing in common with the initial process of concentration for which the soil has been prepared long before, even though it may up to then have been in a latent state. For this reason it is quite possible for a joyful reaction to evoke the composition of a melancholy Largo. The opposite occurs even more often; for sadness can inspire lightness, even gaiety, of musical expression. The work of Haydn and Mozart is full of such instances. The tragedy of Munich, which struck at Martinů's homeland, brought him great unhappiness; yet under its stress he produced one of his most virile works, the Double Concerto.

Thus we see that the original conception remains unchanged in spite of all outside conditions. Indeed, should this not hold true a composer would necessarily have to change his emotional direction many times during the composition of a work, perhaps even in the course of a single movement; and the outcome would be a complete lack of style and structure. After all, the listener at a concert has to receive an impression of a work as a whole, without knowing anything of the conditions — either technical or emotional — under which it was written.

The question may well be asked: what is it that makes music sad or gay? It is quite possible for a piece in a minor key to be of a joyous nature, just as one in the major may be melancholy. Again, what is it that constitutes religious, sensuous, or mystic music? It is impossible to define these things precisely, and what is commonly said on the subject is purely conventional.

When an artist is absorbed in his work, the entire process which preceded it is sublimated and reaffirmed in his mind, becoming part of his daily life, his gestures, his very breath. All his past struggles are forgotten and he knows at last where he stands.

Martinů holds in highest esteem those of his works which came unexpectedly, thus differing in his judgment from the general opinion — that of the critics in particular — which rates higher those immediately following the compositions in which he painfully broke new ground. On the other hand a certain section of the public is apt to demand an emotional and programmatic explanation of an artist's work, not realizing that even in his most dramatic compositions he is usually thinking only of the medium in which he is working, and looking at them from the point of view of his craft. This does not of course mean that when a composer sits down to write a work he is a craftsman only, and that all his ideas are already crystallized and arranged in his mind. But the fact remains that the composer of today, with the present practically unlimited technical resources at his disposal, is necessarily largely occupied with the materialization of his ideas. His imagination must be confined within the boundaries of these material factors, even though they may not always fit in with his original concept. He has to abide by the limitations inherent in the instruments, as well as in sound itself.

Martinů, in spite of the high standard he has set himself, composes very swiftly, even the most complicated parts of his work often being written directly into the master sheet with indelible ink. For this he has as a guide only his practically illegible stenographic pencil notations, as can be seen by the photographs of his sketch for the Second Symphony. The decisive factor in the whole working out is his initial inner process.

Not long ago I asked Martinů what was the most important

element in his creative work. The reply was as simple and deep as the man himself: "Selection and organization." To Martinů the word "selection" is synonymous with "concentration"; and by "organization" he means the clear, organic construction of his work, in which all the components are in functional relation with the whole. Because of the fact that in his own compositions he rejects mediums in general circulation he has been forced to use an entirely different formal structure. He does not, for instance, often employ the form of the sonata, preferring that of the concerto grosso. This is evident even in compositions such as his symphonies, which one might expect to be in sonata form. All compositional ingredients — harmony, polyphony, rhythm, and color — are subordinated to the organic development of the work and its effect as a whole.

It is characteristic of his compositions that the complete theme often does not appear immediately at the beginning of the movement, to be subjected to variation and imitation — as in sonata form — but rather is gradually evolved during the entire movement, so that an unceasing musical current builds up a final unity. Often the treatment of one theme suffices for a movement, without the necessity for a counter-theme. A sense of constructivism plays an important part in his work, as does also a rich and vital rhythmic sense, the latter a Czech and Slovak ingredient. In his latest works this feature is less prominent, as his compositions tend to become more and more lyrical. His sense of orchestration is natural and practically infallible. The sound is always clear, never foggy or merely stormy; and his discoveries in sonority often take the listener by surprise. Martinů draws sharp distinction between the various genres — chamber music, symphonic music, and music for theater and film. His quartet is never an orchestra; his music for the theater is never a symphony. His melody, rhythm, and color emanate directly from the Czech nature; he continues in the footsteps of Dvořák and Smetana.

"His music," wrote Ernest Ansermet recently,[1] is less than most enveloped by æsthetic preventions in that it is based on spirit and truth. What is striking with Martinů," continues the distinguished Swiss conductor, "is the fact that it is impossible to characterize in one word, as it may be in the case of other composers, his melody, which does not represent anything out of the ordinary, his harmony, whose tonal conduct is courageous and complicated but which follows the consecrated path, or his procedure of style. There is, however, one factor which imposes itself, namely the expressive character of his work, which thus is in agreement with the most constant tradition of our art and which Martinů attains through media of his very own. There are only a few composers who have realized their 'mot d'ordre,' *return to pure music*, in so fortunate a manner as his, namely that his composition is fully contained in the musical substance in which he is working and in which he finds a medium enabling him to give his music an ardent life of sentiment without resorting to the rhetoric brought about by romanticism, which became fatally conventional."

The years Martinů spent in Paris, during which his outlook was enriched by the internationalism of the metropolis, clarified his own innately Czech expression. America gave him greater freedom and authority, and an increased craftsmanship in his work. Consequently his compositions are not attached exclusively to local soil, but contribute, rather, as a Czech component, to world culture.

This aim, not only consciously adopted, but part of the composer's very nature, lends his work true originality. It would be an error, however, to suppose that this constitutes

---

[1] In the program notes of Orchestre de la Suisse Romande, November 22, 1943.

a limitation, excluding compositions inspired by deep, passionate, and human feelings. He has written such works, but they never lose balance or control. An example is the Double Concerto, which from first to last is full of emotional tension. In spite of this it does not contain a romantic climax, and is definitely without any "significant substance" — the so-called depth of thought which, as Busoni correctly states, cannot be expressed in musical terms. What is needed today is an unchanging principle of musical beauty and an acknowledgment of the limits of musical expression. These are the foundations of Martinů's entire work.

20 : The Influence of America upon Martinů

DURING the two and a half years of his stay in America Martinů's list of works has been supplemented by fourteen new compositions. Of these six are for orchestra (Concerto da Camera, two symphonies, Violin concerto, Concerto for two pianos, and Memorial to Lidice) ; five are chamber-music works (the Second Cello Sonata, Piano Quartet, Madrigal Sonata, the Variations on a Theme by Rossini, and Madrigal Stanzas) ; two are books of songs (New Špalíček and Songs on One Page) ; and there is one piano composition, the Mazurka — his first work written in America. Although much occupied with all these compositions, as well as by his teaching at the Berkshire Music Center, Martinů has been very receptive to all the new impressions of his visit to the United States. Until now he has made the acquaintance only of the east coast — Washington, Vermont, Massachusetts, and Connecticut. With the exception of ten months in New York City the largest part of this time was spent in the country, close to nature. This fact is important in summing up the influence of America upon Martinů; for he has been strongly affected by the American countryside, finding it more violent in every way than that of Europe, in its climate, its flora and fauna, and its influence on man. His stay on Cape Cod and at Darien, Connecticut, brought him many new impressions and surprises. After the clear air of Czechoslovakia and the mild, kind climate of France, America seems to him very primitive, independent, and free.

Only in a free country, too, would it be possible, at this revolutionary time, to find the perfect books which have given him such a wonderful opportunity to add to his philosophical and scientific reading.[1] However pressed with work, he has always found time to continue the reading which forms so large a part of his interests. Even before he was able to pronounce more than half a dozen words of broken English he had read dozens of books on all phases of scientific thought, including biology and physics. In this is shown his eagerness to add to his incomplete knowledge of mankind and to test and confirm the relationship between his own self-restrained disposition and the outside world. These reading sessions may well prove to be the main influence of America upon Martinů.

Conditions in this country are very different from what he had imagined them to be. His friends in Europe had led him to expect a more or less soulless mechanization; and although he realizes that it is in the solution of technical problems that America leads the world today, he feels their importance is often underestimated in the Old World — even that, in their own way, they represent a spiritual aspect of human existence. In an interesting article published in the New York Czech review *Zítřek* (*Tomorrow*), an organ for Czech writers and

---

[1] The first philosophical book with which Martinů came into contact in America was the English translation of Oswald Spengler's *The Decline of the West*, which he studied in Edgartown, on Martha's Vineyard, in the summer of 1941. Since then he has read a whole series of American books by contemporary philosophers and scientists.

MARTINŮ IN DARIEN, 1943

artists in exile,[2] which asked him to write about his impressions of the United States, he says:

I remember how not so long ago we used to speak of this as the century of mechanization, electricity, speed, and so on . . . and how we called it Americanism and placed it outside the spiritual sphere. *"Mécanisme"* was the name given in those days to all discoveries of the twentieth century.

We of Europe have outgrown the era of the oil lamp; we now press buttons in order to have light. Quite natural, isn't it? We have sometimes felt ourselves to be superior because we have given more time to the solution of metaphysical problems. But in the end we found nothing. As a matter of fact we are still unaware of what may result from technical discoveries. We look upon them as we would admire the tricks of a magician who pulls a white rabbit out of a hat; and we accept as quite natural such marvels as radio and television.

At this point America's part appears in quite another light. We should realize that soon after the war we shall see the results of a technical revolution that will place us in an entirely different situation, from both the social and the spiritual point of view. Questions of health, housing, transit, production — and many others — will be solved right here in this country. (No Schopenhauer, no Spengler.) In reading the report of the National Resource Committee of 1937 we realize in what direction the human brain is working, and see America clearly.

Martinů's interest in modern physics is very great. One of his friends in New York is a young Czech scientist and inventor with whom he regularly spends part of his free time in order to ask questions about such problems as time and space, the principle of uncertainty, and general semantics, which last is connected in America with the name of Alfred Korzybski. They also discuss questions relating to problems of musical sound. Martinů believes with the physicists that it will before long be possible, by means of light and electricity, for a composer to make a direct recording of some of his ideas without the necessity of written scores.

The culture of the Old World, as seen in Paris, while un-

2 Professor O. Odložilík, editor.

doubtedly providing the right atmosphere for Martinů's reflections on the traditions of composition, nevertheless at times deprived him of a certain freedom. It is interesting to note that this was remarked upon by one of America's leading critics — incidentally a great admirer of Martinů's work — when the *Sinfonietta Giocosa*, the last composition Martinů wrote in France, was played in New York. He wrote: "What his work lacks is liberty. It is tight. It says what it says, but it opens not vistas to thought." [3] This is undoubtedly true. It is also true that Martinů is well aware of this lack of liberty, and that he is rapidly losing it here in America. He is, so to speak, emerging from a closed room and beginning to breathe the open air. His advance towards the eternal principles of music and a richer contemporary lyricism, as well as towards folklore, has been noticeably more rapid in this country than in his European period as a whole. Technical problems occupy him less than heretofore; he does not have to force his composition, but keeps it serenely within the scope of a natural and human expression. It is, of course, difficult to say whether this development can be attributed directly to the influence of America or whether it has been merely hastened by better material conditions (including increased possibilities of performance by the better organized orchestras of this country) . That in Paris Martinů had already begun to attain a greater freedom is shown in his opera *Juliette*, an outstanding example of his creative originality. It is also not yet clear to what extent this American liberation has been of advantage to his work; to decide that question we shall have to wait some years in order to be able to appraise it in better perspective. But the fact remains that the works Martinů has composed in the United States appear to be more free, and that they stand out as strongly individual among the immense mass of potential music he accumulated during his many years in Europe, much

---

[3] Virgil Thomson in the *New York Herald Tribune*, March 18, 1942.

of which the conditions of America have given him the opportunity to put into concrete form.

Closely related to this is the question whether Martinů's character manifests itself as more strongly Czech in this country than it did in France. For those who really know his whole work this question does not exist. His more typically Czech compositions — such as *Špaliček* and *Kytice*, to mention only two — are undoubtedly those written in Paris. On the other hand, *Half-Time* and the String Quintet, which are more international in style, were composed in his native town of Polička. Martinů's cosmopolitanism is, paradoxically, a typical expression of his Czech origin. Comenius and Thomas G. Masaryk were cosmopolitan in the same way, as is shown in Masaryk's declaration that the Czech question is a world question in the cultural-political and moral sense of the word. There can be no doubt that Martinů's American period will furnish a chapter of extraordinary interest to the biographer and student of the future. It has not yet reached a definite position; it is still in a state of flux.

There are many sides to Martinů's character, as well as to his intellectual interests; and his visit to America may perhaps satisfy some of these. He is naturally inclined towards generosity, kindness, and friendliness — the basic characteristics of the American people. He has also a Jeffersonian faith in the common man. America, for Martinů, is "something new in history and a successful experiment of intermixture of people and of races." "For the entire history of America," to quote the brilliant formula of the American historians Allan Nevins and Henry Steele Commager, "recapitulates the history of the race, telescopes the social and economic and political institutions." And here, in the land of so many material possibilities for the creative artist, is one who is well aware that a new epoch in the history of man is in preparation.

The future may hold many opportunities for European

artists to work on parallel lines with Americans who — to paraphrase Constance Rourke — cannot take off from the same point of departure as the European artist. Martinů, for instance, may some day utilize American humor by incorporating it into an American opera buffa. Or he may interpret the folklore of America from another angle than that approached fifty years ago by Antonín Dvořák in his use of the Negro spiritual. Martinů's efforts would then be directed to its integration into an absolute musical form which, by carrying its own message, would make it possible not only for America but for the whole world to hear in it the common and eternal values of beauty.

It is certain that Martinů will never write "American music" as such, just as he will never write French or Swiss music. His expression is his very own. If he can be called cosmopolitan, it is in the broader sense of the word, the sense of universal humanity. He has had the opportunity to test the effects of his music on listeners all over the world: in his homeland, in Czechoslovakia, where the public is culturally and spiritually closest to him; in France, where he was forced to break down the barriers raised by his foreign birth; and now in America, where the appreciation of his work has been immediate and spontaneous. The radio, also, in bringing him to the people of all countries, has shown the international response his music is capable of arousing. Martinů, in common with most artists of today, would not wish, even if he were able, to create for a small group of people or for his own nation alone; he must write for all, for mankind as a whole.

In this lies the final criterion of contemporary music, which in its spiritual and technical qualities should be within the reach of all men, without differentiation of race or country. The task of the artist of today is a tremendous one — worthy of Socrates not only in the æsthetic but in the moral sense. At no time in the past has it been of more vital importance.

21 : Speaking of the Man

IN the winter of 1934 I once sat with Martinů at a rehearsal of the opera *The Miracle of Our Lady* in Prague. I saw before me a man changed almost beyond recognition. In everyday life Martinů gives the impression of being shy, polite, indulgent towards the weaknesses of his fellow men; but at the rehearsal he was exactly the opposite. He felt that his intentions regarding the opera were misunderstood, and his criticism was relentless to the point of fury. Finally his expressions became so violent that it was found necessary, in order to avoid a scene, to drop the curtain. The reason for Martinů's anger did not lie in the misinterpretation of details of his work. It was caused by the diametrical opposition between his own conception and that of the stage director, who in the composer's absence had allowed the actors to interpret *The Miracle of Our Lady* as a conventional stereotyped opera, with all the stale theatrical mannerisms that this implies. At that time Martinů had not yet formed his own group of collaborators in Prague, as he later did for his production of *Juliette*. What he wished to attain in the earlier opera was a pure spectacle which should express a given situation without artistic adornment or exaggeration of any kind, as in the scene where Sister Pascaline stands on the scaffold at the moment between life and death. But his anger was aroused because his artistic convictions were disregarded. In those parts of the work where he had reached the greatest sublimity — even a reflection of that universal truth which, in the words of Walter Pater, is "something of the soul of humanity" — the director was aiming at a mere mechanical correctness, in line with his own subjective scale of values.

In these outbursts of justified anger I found the true characteristics of Martinů's personality, his deep convictions, and his artistic greatness of stature. Martinů imagines "intensely and comprehensively," as Shelley expressed it in his *Defence of Poetry*; and his imagination is "the great instrument of moral good, the organ of the moral nature of man." He lays aside his own individuality, divesting himself of all personal uncertainty; and, by putting himself into the place of others in the widest sense, comes into the open and reaches a definite impersonal expression of artistic truth, emotionally as well as rationally.[1] In *The Miracle of Our Lady* Martinů does not portray his personal problems, but those of mankind in general — the moral, intellectual, and emotional values common to all. He is firmly opposed to anything that might separate him from the common man. Everything that the egotism of the artist might bring forward to set himself above his fellow creatures — that is not "along the line of an unselfish devotion to the best," [2] if foreign to him. Martinů's greatest realities lie in the values created by relationships; he agrees with modern philosophy that "no part of the living world can be known by itself alone." [2] He is intensely conscious of all the changes of the present times, believing that we are, in the words of Professor Flewelling, only on "the threshold to yet greater truths of a relational world."

And yet in spite of this quality of impersonal detachment Martinů's work is a full expression of himself. No external mandate, no material difficulties — of which he has had more than his share — have ever been able to divert him from his chosen path and artistic goal. He is not lacking in depth or substance, although, because his work is without those super-

---

[1] I am indebted for some suggestions to the admirable book *The Arts and the Art of Criticism*, by Theodor Meyer Greene (Princeton University Press, 1940).

[2] Ralph Tyler Flewelling: *The Survival of Western Culture* (New York: Harper & Brothers; 1943).

ficial effects and meaningless climaxes which to certain critics imply these qualities, he is sometimes held to be so.

Martinů's own opinion is that his music can best be regarded from the point of view of light. The shadows are created by the angles at which the light is projected upon the subject. It is not necessary to create darkness in order to produce light; quite the contrary. And for Martinů light signifies life — "the total push and pressure of the cosmos," as William James has expressed it. To him it does not include isolationism, analysis of the ego, renunciation, self-pity, or the baring of a deep inaccessible soul. It is energy, strength, pure joy, even humor; and, above all, it is faith and conviction. Martinů is in every way a positive man, and his work a living organism. He possesses what Goethe called *"die exacte Phantasie,"* and is firmly in opposition to all Faustism, skepticism, and irony — in a word, to the entire "superman" complex. The "Demon of the Absolute," which for so long haunted romantic music, does not exist for him.

Martinů is firmly convinced that with the end of the present thirty years' war mankind is approaching a new era; and this is anticipated in his work. He believes that this new era — just as after the crusades — will be happier, more poetic, and more chivalrous; that it will bring the true brotherhood of man. He also feels that after the present crisis the arts will rise in all their grandeur, purity, and beauty. In the cause of this new art — this music for man — Bohuslav Martinů is one of the most humble and faithful of workers.

Martinů's Chief Works

(THIS LIST INCLUDES 124 COMPOSITIONS)

ABBREVIATIONS: 1st P. (First Performance.) — O. P. (Other Performances.)

The place name in parentheses following the title of the work indicates where it was composed.

FOR ORCHESTRA

VANISHING MIDNIGHT (Mizející půlnoc), from the cycle of Three Symphonic Poems, with "The Grove of the Satyrs" and "Shadows" (Prague, 1922). 1st P.: Prague, 1923 (Czech Philharmonic, Václav Talich, conductor). The second and third poems were never performed.

HALF-TIME (Polička, 1925). 1st P.: Prague, 1925 (Czech Philharmonic, Václav Talich, conductor). 2nd P.: Prague, May 17, 1925, at the Festival of the International Society for Contemporary Music. O. P.: Italy, Russia.

LA BAGARRE (Tumult) (Paris, 1926). 1st P.: Boston, November 18 and 19, 1927 (Boston Symphony under Serge Koussevitzky). 2nd P.: broadcast over WBZ–WBZA Westinghouse stations of New England. O. P.: New York, N. Y., Providence, R. I., Prague, Paris, London, Moscow, Stockholm; Italy under Václav Talich.

LA RHAPSODIE (Paris, 1928). 1st P.: Boston, December 14, 1928 (Boston Symphony Orchestra under Serge Koussevitzky). O. P.: Paris (Walther Straram) 1930; Prague (Ernest Ansermet).

LE DÉPART (Paris, 1928). Overture to Act III of the opera Life's Hardships.

Partita (Suite I) for string orchestra (Paris, 1931). Schott. 1st P.: Berlin Radio, 1932. O. P.: New York, 1942 (Alfred Wallenstein's Sinfonietta — radio station WOR); Lyon (France) 1934.

Sinfonia for two orchestras (Paris, 1932).

Overture for the Sokol Festival (Paris, 1932). (Sokol prize-winner.)

INVENTIONS for orchestra (Paris, 1934). 1st P.: Festival of Modern Music, Venice, 1934, O. Piccardi, conductor.

Overture to a Comedy (Suburban Theater) (Paris, 1935). 1st P.: Brno, Czechoslovakia, 1936.

Concerto Grosso for string orchestra, 2 pianos, 2 flutes, 3 oboes, 3 clarinets, 2 horns (Paris 1938). Universal Edition, Vienna. I. Allegro non troppo. II. Lento. III. Allegretto. 1st P.: Boston, November 14, 1941 (Boston Symphony under Serge Koussevitzky). O. P.: New York (Boston Symphony), January 10, 1942; Pittsburgh (Pittsburgh Symphony under Fritz Reiner), December 4, 1942. On this occasion the second movement was dedicated to the memory of the Martyrs of Lidice.

TRE RICERCARI (for 4 violins, 3 cellos, flute, 2 oboes, 2 bassoons, 2 trumpets, 2 pianos) (Paris, 1938). Universal Edition, London. I. Allegro poco. II. Largo. III. Allegro. 1st P.: Venice, 1938, at the Festival of Modern Music. O. P.: Paris, May 8, 1939, at the Triton (Charles Munch with the orchestra of the Société Philharmonique); New York, May 22, 1941, at the 18th Festival of the International Society for Contemporary Music (Alfred Wallenstein with the WOR Sinfonietta).

Double Concerto (2 string orchestras, piano, timpani) (Switzerland 1938). Boosey & Hawkes, New York, London. Duration: 20 minutes. 1st P.: Basel, February 9, 1940 (Paul Sacher and his Kammerorchester). O. P.:

Bern, 1940 (Paul Sacher); Radio Beremuenster, Switzerland, October 2, 1940 (Paul Sacher).

Military March (Paris, 1940). Dedicated to the Czechoslovak Army in France.

Symphony No. 1 (Jamaica, L. I., Middlebury, Vermont, Lenox, Mass., Manomet, Mass., 1942). Boosey & Hawkes, New York, London. Commissioned by the Koussevitzky Music Foundation. Dedicated to Mme Nathalie Koussevitzky. I. Moderato; poco piu mosso. II. Allegro; Trio: poco moderato. III. Largo. IV. Allegro non troppo. 1st P.: Boston, November 13, 1942 (Boston Symphony under Serge Koussevitzky). O. P.: Boston Symphony: Boston, November 14, 1942; New York, November 21, 1942; January 7, 1943.

Symphony No. 2 (Darien, Conn., June 29, 1943–July 24, 1943). Boosey & Hawkes, New York, London. Dedicated to "My Countrymen of Cleveland." I. Allegro moderato (6–8). II. Andante moderato (9–8). III. Poco allegro (2–4). IV. Allegro (4–4). 1st P.: Cleveland, Ohio, October 26 and 28, 1943 (Cleveland Orchestra under Erich Leinsdorf). O. P.: New York (New York Philharmonic Symphony under Artur Rodzinski), December 30 and 31, 1943, January 1, 1944; Pittsburgh, March 17 and 19, 1944 (Pittsburgh Symphony under Fritz Reiner); Minneapolis, April 7, 1944 (Minneapolis Symphony Orchestra under D. Mitropoulos).

MEMORIAL TO LIDICE (Darien, Conn., August, 1943). 1st P.: New York, October 28, 1943 (New York Philharmonic Symphony under Artur Rodzinski in commemoration of the 25th anniversary of the Czechoslovak Republic). O. P.: Philadelphia, Dec. 3, and 5, 1943 (Philadelphia Orchestra under Eugene Ormandy).

FOR SOLO INSTRUMENTS AND ORCHESTRA

Piano Concerto No. 1 (Polička, 1925). Dedicated to Jan Heřman. 1st P.:

Prague, 1926 (Czech Philharmonic under Václav Talich, with Jan Heřman as soloist). O. P.: Paris, February 11, 1928 (at the Concerts Colonne under Gabriel Pierné, with Lucette Descaves as soloist); Paris, 1930, Société des Concerts du Conservatoire (Philippe Gaubert, same soloist).

Concertino for left hand with chamber orchestra (Paris, 1928).

Concerto for violoncello and chamber orchestra (Paris, 1931). Schott. (Transcribed for full orchestra, Paris, 1939.) Dedicated to and first performed by G. Cassado in Berlin. O. P.: Radio Prague; Radio Strasbourg; Paris, 1939 (Société Philharmonique under Charles Munch, with Pierre Fournier as soloist).

String Quartet with orchestra (Paris, 1931). Schott. I. Allegro vivo (2–2). II. Adagio (4–4). III. Finale. Tempo moderato (2–4). 1st P.: London, October 1932 (Pro Arte Quartet with London Philharmonic Orchestra, at a Courtauld-Sargent concert). O. P.: Boston, December 23, 1932 (Richard Burgin, Robert Gundersen, Jean Lefranc, Jean Bedetti, with Boston Symphony under Serge Koussevitzky). New York City, April 9, 1936 (Pro Arte Quartet with the New York Philharmonic Symphony under Hans Lange); 1942 (WQXR Quartet with National Orchestral Association under Leon Barzin). Brussels, 1932; Vienna, 1936; Los Angeles, 1942 (Pro Arte).

Concerto for violin (Paris, 1932). Unfinished and lost. Dedicated to Samuel Dushkin.

Concertino for piano trio and orchestra (Paris, 1933). 1st P.: Basel, 1936 (Paul Sacher with Kammerorchester). O. P.: Paris, 1936 (Triton).

Piano concerto No. 2 (Paris, 1935). Written for and dedicated to Germaine Leroux. I. Allegro poco moderato (4–4). II. Poco andante (6–4). III. Allegro con brio (2–4). Reorchestrated in New York, January 1944. *1st P.*: Prague, 1935 (Czech Philharmonic with Rudolf Firkušný, by special permission of Germaine Leroux). *O. P.*: With Germaine Leroux: Radio Luxembourg, 1936; Paris, January 31, 1937 (Société de Concerts du Conservatoire, Philippe Gaubert); Radio Paris, February 2, 1937 (Fritz Zweig); Glasgow, December 25, 1937 (Scottish Orchestra, George Szell); Prague, April 1938 (Czech Philharmonic, K. B. Jirák); Bucharest, January 1938 (Bucharest Philharmonic, N. Jora); New York, January 24, 1940 (New York Philharmonic Symphony, Herman Adler); Newark, N. J., January 22, 1941 (New Jersey Philharmonic, Henri Pensis). With Rudolf Firkušný: London, November 15, 1938 (Czech Philharmonic, Rafael Kubelík); Lima, Peru, August 20, 1943 (Orquesta Sinfónica Nacional, Theo Buchwald); New York, November 24, 1943 (CBS Symphony Orchestra, Bernard Hermann).

Concerto for harpsichord and chamber orchestra (Paris, 1935). Dedicated to Marcelle de Lacour.

Concerto for flute, violin, and orchestra (Paris, 1936). *1st P.*: Paris, 1936 (Société des Concerts du Conservatoire, Philippe Gaubert, with Marcel Moise, flute, and Blanche Honegger, violin, as soloists).

Concertino for piano and orchestra (Paris, 1937).

Due Concertante for 2 violins and orchestra (Paris, 1937).

Suite Concertante for violin and orchestra (Paris, 1937); revised New York, 1942. Dedicated to Samuel Dushkin. Arranged for violin and piano by Erich Etor Kahn. *1st P.*: New York, 1943, Samuel Dushkin's Town Hall recital (with piano).

Sonata da camera for violoncello and chamber orchestra (Aix-en-Provence, 1940). Dedicated to Henri Honegger. *1st P.*: Basel, 1940 (Paul Sacher with his Kammerorchester and H. Honegger as soloist). *2nd P.*: Ge-

neva, 1942 (same orchestra, same soloist). *O. P.*: Geneva, November 22, 1943 (E. Ansermet with Orchestre de la Suisse Romande, same soloist.)

SINFONIETTA GIOCOSA for piano and chamber orchestra (Aix-en-Provence, October–November 1940; revised in Pleasantville, N. Y., 1941). Boosey & Hawkes, New York, London. Duration: 30 minutes. Written for and dedicated to Germaine Leroux. (*"Le dernier cadeau de France."*) I. Poco Allegro (4–4). II. Allegretto moderato (2–4). III. Allegro (4–8). IV. Andantino (2–8); Allegro (2–4). *1st P.*: New York, March 16, 1942 (National Orchestral Association under Leon Barzin, with Germaine Leroux as soloist).

Concerto da camera for violin and string orchestra (with piano and timpani) (Edgartown, Mass., 1941). I. Moderato, poco allegro (6–8). II. Adagio (6–4). III. Poco Allegro (Cadenza) (3–4). *1st P.*: Basel, January 1942 (Paul Sacher with Kammerorchester and Gertrude Flügel as soloist).

Concerto for 2 pianos and orchestra (New York, 1943). I. Allegro non troppo (3–4). II. Adagio (without time signature). III. Allegro (3–8). *1st P.*: Philadelphia, November 5, 6, 1943 (Philadelphia Orchestra under Eugene Ormandy, with Luboschutz and Nemenoff as soloists). *O. P.*: New York, November 9, 1943 (same orchestra, same soloists); Los Angeles, March 1944 (Jansen Symphony, same soloists).

Concerto for violin and orchestra (New York, 1943). Written for and dedicated to Mischa Elman. I. Andante, Poco Allegro; Andante. II. Poco Moderato. III. Poco Allegro. *1st P.*: Boston, December 31, 1943 and January 1, 1944 (Boston Symphony under Serge Koussevitzky, with Mischa Elman as soloist). *O. P.*: New York, January 6 and 8, 1944 (same orchestra, same soloist).

122

FOR CHAMBER ORCHESTRA

ENTR'ACTE — Three pieces for chamber orchestra (Paris, 1928). *1st P.*: Baden-Baden Musical Festival, 1928.

Suite from the ballet REVUE DE CUISINE (Suite for jazz) (Paris, 1928). Leduc, Paris. *1st P.*: Paris, 1928, at Cortot Concerts (Dinan Alexanian, conductor).

Serenade for chamber orchestra (18 instruments) (Paris, 1930). Schott. *1st P.*: Paris (Straram Orchestra, 1931). *O. P.*: Prague (V. Talich), Lyon (Witkowski), Geneva (E. Ansermet).

LES RONDES (Paris, 1932). *1st P.*: Cortot Concerts at the École Normale de musique, 1932.

See also under "For Solo Instruments and Orchestra": Concerto for violoncello and chamber orchestra, Paris, 1931 (original version). Concertino for left hand with chamber orchestra. Concerto for harpsichord and chamber orchestra. Sonata da camera for violoncello and chamber orchestra. *Sinfonietta giocosa* for piano and chamber orchestra. Concerto da camera for violin and string orchestra (with piano and timpani).

CHAMBER MUSIC

String Quartet No. 1 (Prague, 1921). MS. *1st P.*: Prague, 1928 (Ševčík Quartet).

String Quartet No. 2 (Paris, 1926). Universal Edition, Vienna. *1st P.*: Berlin, 1927 (Novák-Frank Quartet). *O. P.*: Paris, 1927; Festival of Baden-Baden, 1927 (Amar Quartet); Festival of I.S.C.M. at Siena, September 15, 1928; Vienna (Coolidge Quartet).

Duo for Violin and Violoncello (Paris, 1927). Sirène Musicale, Paris. *1st P.*: Paris, 1927 (Novák-Frank). *O. P.*: Prague; Warsaw; Berlin; New York, February 21, 1941 and March 27, 1942 (Bernard Ocko and Lucien L. Kirsch). Record: French Columbia C–DFX½ (O. Rithère and M. Huvelin).

String Quintet (Polička, 1927) (2 violins, 2 violas, violoncello). I. Allegro con brio. II. Largo. III. Allegretto (non troppo). *1st P.*: Pittsfield, Mass., 1928 (Elizabeth Sprague Coolidge Chamber Music Festival). *O. P.*: Paris; London; Geneva; Warsaw; Prague; Zürich; Washington, August 18, 1943 (Britt String Ensemble).

Quintet for wind ensemble (Paris, 1930).

Five short pieces for violin and piano (Paris, 1930). Leduc, Paris.

ARABESQUES for violoncello and piano (Paris, 1930). Leduc.

NOCTURNES for violoncello and piano (Paris, 1930). Leduc.

Trio for violin, violoncello, and piano (*Cinq Pièces brèves*) (Paris, 1930). Schott. *1st P.*: Paris, 1931 (Trio Belge). *O. P.*: Paris, 1933 (Trio Hongrois) at the Triton.

String Sextet (2 violins, 2 violas, 2 violoncellos) (Coolidge Prize, 1932) (Paris, May 20–7, 1932). I. Lento — Allegro poco moderato. II. Andantino — Allegro scherzando — Tempo I. III. Allegretto poco moderato. *1st P.*: Washington, April 24, 1933 (Library of Congress, Festival of Chamber Music) by Kroll Sextet (William Kroll, Nicolas Berezovsky, Leon Barzin, O. Saltisow, Milton Prinz, and Ossip Giskin).

Sonatine for 2 violins and piano (Paris, 1931). Leduc. *1st P.*: London (Sonata Players).

Sonata No. 1 for violin and piano (Paris, 1931). Leduc.

Études rythmiques for violin and piano (Paris, 1931). Schott.

Duos for 2 violins (2 books) (Paris, 1931). Leduc.

String Quartet No. 3 (Paris, 1932). Leduc. *1st P.*: Paris (Triton).

Études rythmiques for violin (Paris, 1931). Leduc.

Études rythmiques for violoncello (Paris, 1931). Leduc.

Arietta for violoncello and piano (Paris, 1932).

Sonata for 2 violins and piano (Paris,

1932). Deiss, Paris. Written for the Sonata Players, London.

Sonata No. 2 for violin and piano (Paris, 1933). Deiss.

Piano Quintet (Paris, 1934). Sirène Musicale. *1st P.*: Switzerland. *O. P.*: London, New York, March 7, 1937 (Pro Arte Quartet and Irene Jacobi) for the American League of Composers.

String Trio (Paris, 1936). Written and dedicated to Trio Pasquier. *1st P.*: Náchod, Czechoslovakia, October 1937.

String Quartet No. 4 (Paris, 1936).

Sonata for flute, violin, and piano (Paris, 1936). Dedicated to Marcel Moyse. French His Master's Voice, Record G–L 104⅞ (M. Moyse, B. Honegger, L. Moyse).

LES MADRIGAUX for oboe, clarinet, bassoon (Paris, 1937).

String Quartet No. 5 (Paris, 1938). Written for and dedicated to Pro Arte Quartet.

Sonatine for violin and piano (Paris, 1938). Pro Musica, Prague.

Sonata No. 1 for violoncello and piano (Paris, 1940).

PROMENADES for flute, violin, and harpsichord (Paris, 1940).

BERGERETTES for violin, violoncello, and piano (Paris, 1940).

Sonata No. 2 for violoncello and piano (New York, 1941). Associated Music Publishers, New York. *1st P.*: New York, March 27, 1942 (Lucien L. Kirsch and Elly Bontempo).

Piano Quartet (Jamaica, L. I., New York (1942). I. Poco allegro. II. Adagio. III. Allegretto. IV. Poco moderato. *1st P.*: Berkshire Music Center, Lenox, Mass., August 1942. *O. P.*: New York, March 2, 1943, at the "First Serenade" (Chamber Music Guild Quartet).

Madrigal Sonata for flute, violin, and piano (New York, October 9 and 19, 1942). I. Poco allegro. II. Moderato. III. Allegro. Salute to the League of Composers in celebration of the League's Twentieth Anniversary. *1st P.*: New York, December 9, 1942 at

the Town Hall (Ruth Freeman, Roman Totenberg, Elly Bontempo). *O. P.*: Radio Station WQXR, 1943.

Variations on a Theme of Rossini for violoncello (New York, 1942). Dedicated to Gregor Piatigorsky. *1st P.*: May 1943, Frick Museum (Gregor Piatigorsky).

Madrigal Stanzas (five pieces) for violin and piano (New York, November 1943). Dedicated to Albert Einstein.

SOLO COMPOSITIONS FOR PIANO AND HARPSICHORD

PUPPETS I (*Loutky I*) (Prague, 1908). Published by Chadim Prague.

PUPPETS II (*Loutky II*) (Prague, 1909). Urbánek, Prague.

FILM EN MINIATURE (Paris, 1926). Éd. Hudební Matice, Prague.

TROIS DANSES TCHÈQUES (Paris, 1925). Eschig, Paris; Schott. Obkročák. Dupák. Polka.

PRÉLUDES (Paris, 1931). Leduc.

BOROVÁ (Danses tchèques) (Paris, 1931). Leduc.

ESQUISSES DE DANSE (5 pièces) (Paris, 1932). Schott. Performed in New York on November 25, 1940 at Town Hall recital of Germaine Leroux.

Pièce pour piano (in *Album des auteurs modernes*) (Paris, 1932). Sirène Musicale, Paris, 1932.

LES RITOURNELLES (6 pièces) (Paris, 1932). Schott, 1933. Performed in New York on December 14, 1941 at the Town Hall recital by Rudolf Firkušný.

Dumka for piano (in the volume *Klavír 1937*) (Paris, 1936). Hudební Matice, Prague, 1937.

2 Preludes for harpsichord (Paris, 1935). Dedicated to Marcelle de Lecour.

THE WINDOW IN THE GARDEN (*Okna do zahrady*) Five pieces. (Vieux Moulin [near Paris], 1938).

TRAIN HANTÉ (Album for Marguerite Long) (Paris, 1938).

Fantaisie and Rondo (Aix-en-Provence, 1940). Dedicated to Rudolf Firkušný. *1st P.*: New York, February 2,

1943. *O. P.*: 1943: Buenos Aires, Rio de Janeiro, Santiago de Chile, Montevideo.
Mazurka for piano (Paderewski Memorial) (Album). *1st P.*: Paderewski Memorial, New York (Rudolf Firkušný).

OPERAS

THE SOLDIER AND THE DANCER (*Voják a Tanečnice*), three acts, libretto by J. L. Budín (Paris, 1926–7). *1st P.*: National Theater, Brno, 1928.
THE TEARS OF THE KNIFE (*Les Larmes du couteau*), one act, libretto by Ribemont-Dessaignes (Paris, 1928).
LIFE'S HARDSHIPS (*Les Vicissitudes de la vie*), three acts, with film, libretto by Ribemont-Dessaignes (Paris, 1928). (Unfinished.)
THE DAY OF KINDNESS (*Journeé de bonté*), three acts, libretto by Ilja Ehrenburg, B. Martinů, and Ribemont-Dessaignes (Paris, 1929).
THE MIRACLE OF OUR LADY (*Hry o Marii*), four parts, libretto by B. Martinů and Henri Ghéon (Paris, 1933). *1st P.*: National Theater, Brno, 1934 (Antonín Balatka, conducting; Dr. Branko Gavela, stage director). *O. P.*: Prague, National Theater, March 1935 (J. Charvát, conducting).
THE SUBURBAN THEATER (*Divadlo za bránou*), three acts, opera buffa, libretto by B. Martinů (Paris, 1935). Performed in 1936 by the National Theater, Brno.
ALEXANDRE BIS, one act, libretto by André Wormser (Paris, 1937).
JULIETTE, OR THE KEY TO DREAMS, three acts, libretto by Georges Neveux (Paris, 1936–7). *1st P.*: Prague, National Theater, February 1938 (Václav Talich, conducting; Jindřich Honzl, stage director; František Muzika, designs).

OPERAS AND CANTATA FOR RADIO

THE VOICE OF THE FOREST (*Hlas lesa*), 30 minutes, libretto by V.

Nezval (Paris, 1935)—six voices, one narrator, chamber orchestra. *1st P.*: Prague Radio, 1935.
COMEDY ON A BRIDGE (*Komedie na mostě*), 45 minutes (Paris, 1937)—five voices, 3 narrators, chamber orchestra. *1st P.*: Prague Radio, 1937.
BOUQUET OF FLOWERS (*Kytice*), cantata for solos, chorus, chamber orchestra, and two pianos; 50 minutes; Czech folk poetry (Paris, 1938). (Two parts.) Sestra travička. Halékání. Milá nad rodinu. Koleda. Člověk a smrt. *1st P.*: Radio Prague, 1938.

BALLETS

ISTAR, 3 acts (Prague, 1921). *1st P.*: National Theater, Prague, 1922.
WHO IS THE MOST POWERFUL IN THE WORLD? (*Kdo je na světě nejmocnější?*) one act (ballet of animals) (Prague, 1923). *1st P.*: National Theater, Brno, 1924.
REVOLT (*Vzpoura*), one act (Paris, 1925). *1st P.*: National Theater, Brno, 1926.
ON TOURNE, one act (Paris, 1925).
THE KITCHEN REVUE (La Revue de cuisine) (*Kuchyňská revue*), one act (Paris, 1927). *1st P.*: Prague, Umělecká Beseda (Group of Jarmila Kröschlová; Stanislav Novák, conducting).
LE RAID MERVEILLEUX (ballet méchanique) (Paris, 1927–8).
CHECKMATING THE KING (*Echec au Roi*), one act, argument by André Cœuroy (Paris, 1928.)
THE BUTTERFLY THAT STAMPED (*Motýl, který dupal*), one act, based on R. Kipling (Paris, 1929.)
ŠPALÍČEK, Czech ballet in three acts, with women's chorus (Paris, 1931). *1st P.*: Prague, 1932, National Theater.
THE JUDGMENT OF PARIS (*Le Jugement de Paris*), one act (Paris, 1935).

CANTATAS AND OTHER VOCAL WORKS

NIPPONARI for voice and seven instruments (Prague, 1908).

CHILDREN'S SONGS (*Dětské písně*) (Polička, 1916).

MAGIC NIGHTS (*Kouzelné noci*), for voice and orchestra (Prague, 1919). Dedicated to Drill Oridge.

CZECH RHAPSODY (*Česká rapsodie*) for orchestra, organ, solos, and mixed chorus (Prague, 1918). *1st P.*: Prague, 1919 (Czech Philharmonic under L. V. Čelanský).

Two Songs to folk texts for contralto and piano (Paris, 1929).

VOCALISE EN FORME D'ARIETTE (Paris, 1930). Leduc.

SONGS OF MARY (*Písně o Marii*), for women's chorus, on folk texts (Paris, 1936).

Three Fragments from the opera JULIETTE (for concert performance), 5 solos: soprano, alto, tenor, baritone, bass; and orchestra (Paris, 1938). 45 minutes. I. Souvenirs. II. Forest scene. III. Finale.

MADRIGALS for six women voices (Czech folk legends) (Paris, 1938).

FIELD MASS (*La Messe aux champs d'honneur*) for male chorus, baritone solo, and orchestra (2 piccolos, two clarinets, three trumpets, two trombones, piano, harmonium, drums) (Paris, 1939).

NEW ŠPALÍČEK, Songs for voice and piano on Czech folk poetry (Jamaica, L. I., 1942).

SONGS ON ONE PAGE (*Písničky na jednu stránku*), seven songs (New York, 1943). Dedicated to Mme Olga Hurban.

MUSIC FOR FILM

UNFAITHFUL MARIJKA (*Marijka nevěrnice*), based on Ivan Olbracht's novel (Prague, 1935). Vladislav Vančura, film director.

Bibliography

Here are listed some of the books which have been useful to me.

BEKKER, PAUL: *The Changing Opera* (W. W. Norton, New York, 1935)

BERENCE, FRED: *Raphaël, ou la puissance de l'esprit.* (Éd. Plon, Paris)

COMMAGER, HENRY STEELE, and NEVINS, ALLAN: *The Pocket History of the United States.* (Pocket Books, Inc., New York)

CONKLIN, EDWIN GRANT: *Man: Real and Ideal.* (New York, Charles Scribner's Sons, 1943)

COPLAND, AARON: *Our New Music.* Leading composers in Europe and America. (New York, Whittlesey House, 1941)

DEWEY, JOHN: *Art as Experience.* (Milton, Balch & Company, New York, 1934)

EINSTEIN, ALFRED: *Greatness in the Music.* (Oxford University Press, New York, London, Toronto, 1924)

FLEWELLING, RALPH TYLER: *The Survival of Western Culture.* (Harper & Brothers, New York, 1943)

GREEN, THEODORE MEYER: *The Arts and the Art of Criticism.* (Princeton University Press, 1940)

HROMÁDKA, J. L.: *Don Quichote of the Czech Philosophy.* New York, 1943.

International Cyclopedia of Music and Musicians. Edited by Oscar Thompson (Dodd, Mead & Co., New York, 1939)

JAKOBSON, ROMAN: *Wisdom of the Old Czechs.* (Published in Czech, by the Czechoslovak Cultural Circle, New York, 1943)

MULLER, HERBERT J.: *Science and Criticism.* The Humanistic Tradition in Contemporary Thought. (Yale University Press, 1943)

PATER, WALTER: *Appreciations.* (Macmillan, London, 1895)

PÉGUY, CHARLES: *Basic Verities.* Prose and Poetry. (Pantheon Books, Inc., New York, 1943)

REISER, OLIVER L.: *The Promise of Scientific Humanism.* Toward a Unification of Scientific, Religious, Social and Economic Thought. (Oscar Piest, New York, 1940)

ROURKE, CONSTANCE: *The Roots of American Culture.* (New York, Harcourt, Brace & Co., 1942)

SCHLUMBERGER, JEAN: *Jalons* (Brentanos', New York, 1941)

SEARS, PAUL B.: *This Is Our World.* (University of Oklahoma Press)

——: *Deserts on the March.* (University of Oklahoma Press)

TOVEY, DONALD FRANCIS: *Essays in Musical Analysis.* Vol. III. Concertos. (Oxford University Press, 1936)

Index

i

INDEX

INDEX

INDEX

INDEX

Music: of sixteenth, seventeenth, eighteenth centuries, ix; impersonal, 35
Musical Quarterly, 89
Musset, Alfred de, 63
Muzika, František, 125

National Orchestral Association, 39, 78, 121, 122
National Resource Committee, 113
National Theater, Brno, 53
National Theater, Prague, 10, 17, 23, 57
Nativity, 57
Negro spiritual, 116
Neo-classical music, 38
Neo-classicism, ix
Nettl, Paul, xii
Neumann, František, 53
Neveux, Georges, 63
Nevins, Allan, 115
New German Theater, 10
New Špalíček, 83, 111
New York Herald Tribune, 45, 91, 102, 114
New York Philharmonic Symphony, 39, 95, 102, 121, 122
New York Times, 37, 45
New York World-Telegram, 45
New Yorské Listy, 21, 45, 71, 73
Nezval, Vítězslav, 56, 125
Nietzsche, ix
Nikolska, Jelizaveta, 17
Niponari, 9, 125
Novák, Stanislav, 12, 13, 31, 125
Novák-Frank, Quartet, 31, 123
Novotná, Jarmila, 83

Ocko, Bernard, 123
Ogolovets, A. S., 85
Olbracht, Ivan, 126
On Tourne, 125
Opera: the laws and logic of, 60; buffa, 79
Opera film, 52
Operatic form, origin of, 60
Orchestre de la Suisse Romande, 110, 122
Orel, D., 85
Oridge, Drill, 10, 126
Oriental texts, 9
Ormandy, Eugene, 101, 102, 121, 122
Orquesta Sinfónica Nacional, 122

Overture: for the Sokol Festival, 120; to a Comedy, 120

Paderewski Memorial, 82
Palestrina, ix
Pantomime, 52
Parc Montsouris, 43
Paris, vii, 18, 19, 20, 21, 28
Paris Philharmonic, 40
Parry, Hubert H., 86
Partita, 40, 120
Pastiches, of old masters, 38
Pater, Walter, 117
Péguy, Charles, 30
Père Gogo, 75
Persinger, Louis, 37
Phantom Bridegroom, Legend of the, 56
Philadelphia Orchestra, 101, 121, 122
Phonograph records, xii
Physics, vii, 102
Piano Concertos: No. 1, 121; No. 2, 40, 121
Piano Quartets, 86, 111, 124
Piatigorsky, Gregor, 101
Pierné, Gabriel, 121
Pierrot, 63
Pirandello, 15
Pittsburgh Symphony, 120, 121
Plautus, 51
Pleasantville, N. Y., 82
Polička, 2, 4, 6, 7, 8, 14, 15, 20, 23, 27, 50, 115
Polyphonic activity, 44
Polyphony, 22, 34, 35, 36, 38, 44
Poussin, 22
"Prague Concertos," 38
Préludes, 124
Přemysl Otakar II, 4
Prinz, Milton, 123
Pro Arte Quartet, 39, 121
Promenades, 124
Providence, R. I., 120
Prunières, Henri, 41
Przybyszewski, Stanislaw, 8
Psalms, 74
Puppets, 32, 124
Puss in Boots, Tale of, 55
Pyrenees, 77

Quais of the Seine, 20
Qualities, permanent, of man, ix
Quatrocentists, x

V

INDEX

This book is set in Electra, a Linotype face designed by W. A. Dwiggins. This face cannot be classified as either modern or old-style. It is not based on any historical model, nor does it echo any particular period or style. It avoids the extreme contrast between thick and thin elements that marks most modern faces, and attempts to give a feeling of fluidity, power, and speed.

The book was composed, printed, and bound by THE PLIMPTON PRESS, Norwood, Massachusetts.